THE MOVEABLE FLEET

THE
MOVEABLE FLEET
A BOATWATCHER'S GUIDE TO SAN FRANCISCO BAY

BY GERALD GEORGE AND MOLLIE RIGHTS

A California Living Book

*To the Bay's watermen and waterwomen
and
those who watch them.*

Design by Jill Anthony

Production by David Charlsen

Cover photo by Gene Anthony

First Edition
Copyright © 1979 California Living Books
The San Francisco Examiner
Division of The Hearst Corporation.
Suite 223, The Hearst Building,
Third and Market Streets,
San Francisco, California 94103

Printed in the United States of America.

ISBN 0-89395-016-5

Library of Congress Catalog Card Number
78-75162

Contents

	Page
Acknowledgments	6
Introduction	7
Salty Talk	10
Merchant Shipping	13
Ports of the Bay	15
Shipyards	16
Shipping Schedule	17
Hull Design	18
Engines	20
Propellers	21
Tonnage and Displacement	22
Ship's Markings	23
Liquid Cargo Carriers	24
Supertankers	25
General Purpose Cargo Ships	30
Container Ships	32
Roll-on/Roll-off Ships	34
Dry Cargo Carriers	36
Hybrid Ships	37
Specialized Carriers	38
Passenger Ships	40

	Page
Navy	43
Tugs, Towboats, and Barges	49
Oceangoing Tugs	53
Harbor Tugs	55
Towboats	59
Barges	60
Workboats	64
Of Pilots and Their Boats	64
Cranes	70
Research Vessels	71
Coast Guard	73
Passenger Vessels	77
Ferries	77
Charter Cruises	79

	Page
Fishing Boats	81
Salmon Trolling	82
Albacore Trolling	83
Long Lining	85
Draggers	86
Lampara Net	88
Crab Boats	90
Historical Ships	92
Pleasure Boats	101
Sailboats	102
Motorsailers	107
Power	108
Where to Watch Boats	111
San Francisco	111
Oakland	117
Alameda	120
Marin County	121
Richmond	123
North Bay	124
Index	126

Acknowledgments

It's hard to know where to begin acknowledging all of the assistance that has made this book possible. The men and women who keep the Bay's maritime world moving have patiently answered countless sincere, but sometimes silly, questions. No matter where the man in the derby and the lady in the Spanish hat went, we found friendly, knowledgeable, and helpful people. For all the facts, the stories, and all the hot coffee, we are forever in their debt.

The scope of this book has required gathering information from diverse sources. In sorting out the complexities of merchant shipping we were helped by: Gary Hallin, Maritime Administration; Captains Donald Grant and Mike Simenstad, San Francisco Bar Pilots; Inland Pilot Captain Bob Atthowe; Tom Walsh, States Line; Tom Wyman, Chevron Shipping Company; Exxon Shipping; Bob Lawson, Norsk Pacific Lines; Jan Loeff, Sitmar Cruises; Princess Cruises; Royal Viking Line; Captain Smith and Pete Schumaker, United States Line; California Maritime Academy; Robert Langner, Marine Exchange; Charles Regal, Matson Navigation Company; and Meredith Peters, Delta Lines.

Other sections of the book were helped immeasurably by: Captain Earl Jensen, California Launch Service; Bob Van Amburg, Harbor Tours; Paul Gordenev, Western Pacific Railroad; D. Ross Sullivan, Santa Fe Railroad; John Esterheld, Marin Yacht Sales; Les Bedient, Roy Nichols, and Annie Reutinger, Crowley Maritime Corporation; Chris Dann, Ocean Trust Foundation; "Sam" Tarantino; John and his helpful, cheerful sons at Frank's Fishing; Meatball and the crew of *Buccaneer*; Marie DeSantis; Steve, John, and Frank of *Condor*; Betty Mann; Faith Tamarin; Sandy, Mike, Barnaby, and everybody at the Pier 9 office, Western Tug; Captain Reno Matilla and his crew on *Siegfried Tiger*; Captain Walt Holck and the crew of *Coyote*; William Angelloni, Army Corps of Engineers; Edward Conlon, U.S. Coast Guard; Manuel Lehue, Blaine Hardy, and the valiant crew of the fireboat *Phoenix*; Steve Mann; Port of Oakland; and J.D. Tikalsky, Navy Public Affairs Office.

We would like to extend special gratitude to: Chong Lee and his lab for their fine photographic prints; Shirley and Al Kohlwes for many things; Hal Silverman for confidence; and Jill Anthony because she finds joy in many things and enjoys sharing.

Introduction

High in a tower of commerce in San Francisco's financial district a blue-suited man with graying temples listens as his subordinates review a pending merger. He hears but doesn't hear because his attention has been drawn out through the window to the sparkling blue Bay. At a waterfront café a young waitress asks her customers to repeat their orders in a voice that indicates she is not entirely there. A jogger on the Embarcadero runs right into a police officer bolting down his lunch. These unfortunate people, and untold thousands like them, are boat-watchers. They are hopelessly addicted to an activity almost as old as technology itself. Corporate barons, political states-men, street sweepers, baseball players, and people from all walks of life share their compulsion. They are dreamers, romantics, vicarious voyagers on the oceans of the mind. There are no national institutes to help them, no benevolent societies to lead them from temptation. There are only books like this, written by fellow sufferers, which promise only to make things worse.

Addictive or not, boatwatching is fun, nonfattening, and informative. The San Francisco Bay Area is a particularly good place to boatwatch because of the number of boats on the Bay and the abundance of places to watch them from. More than a hundred thousand pleasure boats sail the San Francisco Bay; almost ten thousand commercial ships transit these waters each year with cargo from all over the world. Added to those two groups are the countless fish-ing boats, work boats, tugs, ferries, tour boats, launches — the list keeps going, because the selection of boats to watch is unusually concentrated on the marvel-ous San Francisco Bay.

San Francisco Bay

From the sea it can be deceiving. High cliffs and jagged rocks continuously awash in thundering mist conceal its almost cavernous entrance, the place John Charles Fremont called "The Golden Gate." But inside that narrow gate is the largest natural landlocked harbor in the world. Four hundred fifty square miles in area, San Francisco Bay is so large that only satellites and high-flying aircraft can see it all.

The Bay is a creature of many moods. It can be calm and sunny, blustering or shrouded in fog. With a touch of provin-ciality, many Bay sailors maintain that if you can sail on San Francisco Bay you can sail anywhere. Winds from different directions and speeds are common. Fifty-knot gusts can be guaranteed in the winter, and what you find in one place is sure to change around the corner. Like the winds, the currents change in force and direction, depending on location and tides. Then there is the fog, at times so thick you can't see your own bow. But to most people who live, work, or play on

7

it, San Francisco Bay is a jewel — an emerald set among jade hills. There is no other place like it on earth.

As geologists measure such things, the Bay is rather young, less than a million years old. Before there was a Bay, two parallel ranges of mountains had risen to create a valley between them. The mighty Sacramento River carved down through the rising barriers to maintain its access to the sea, creating the Carquinez Strait through the eastern range and the Golden Gate through the western range. Glaciers were upon the land, and sea level was three hundred feet lower than it is today. In time the climate changed, the glaciers melted, and the sea level rose, sending tendrils through the Golden Gate to drown the valley. Where the valley had been deep the young Bay remained deep, but along its shallow margins river-borne mud accumulated. Marshes sprang up in the shallow places, trapping still more mud, and to them

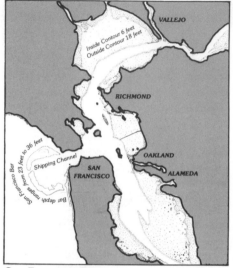

San Francisco Bay

came millions of migratory water birds.

Man and his boats came later. The first mariners were the Indians who made vessels from the tule, or large bulrushes, that grow in the marshy margins of the Bay. These vessels were more barges than boats, not well suited for the open Bay. Then came the Spanish, who established ranchos in the hills around

the Bay. Boats were the colonist's primary means of communication with the village at Yerba Buena Cove, now San Francisco's financial district. They called it the Bay of Saint Francis, after the patron saint of travelers. Toward the end of the rancho period, American whalers and merchant ships began to frequent the Bay.

But it wasn't until 1849, when the lust for gold brought thousands of people to California, that the Bay's potential as a world port was realized. Once it began, however, the transformation was almost immediate. The central Bay became crowded with fast-sailing clipperships. Piers were hastily built. Paddle wheelers churned up and down the rivers beneath black clouds of smoke. Soon there were also fishing boats, water taxis, tugs, hay scows, and an almost infinite variety of other craft, each with its own role to play. The Bay became what it is today, a bustling world of maritime commerce.

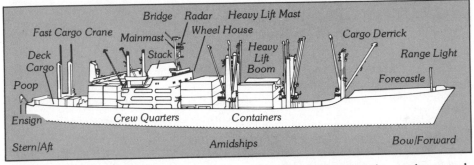

The image labels the parts of a cargo ship: Poop, Deck Cargo, Fast Cargo Crane, Mainmast, Stack, Bridge, Wheel House, Radar, Heavy Lift Mast, Heavy Lift Boom, Cargo Derrick, Range Light, Forecastle, Ensign, Crew Quarters, Containers, Stern/Aft, Amidships, Bow/Forward.

Boatwatching

The first time you cast your eyes on San Francisco Bay to look at boats rather than at the splendid scenery can be overwhelming. The number and variety of craft seem so bewildering that only a professional boat person could sort them out. Don't be discouraged. You will probably be able to differentiate more than you think, once you recover from the discovery of just how busy the Bay is.

Size is the first thing that becomes apparent. Tankers are huge in relation to the tugs and water taxis that service them. Ship people consider the difference important. Though they often call their own vessels "boats," they can get testy when an outsider does the same thing. *Boat* is a term used for smaller watercraft in general. Ship sailors sometimes look at it less technically, proclaiming "boats are carried on ships." That too is generally true, but there are exceptions to both criteria.

Lake, river, and excursion vessels, ferries and submarines, regardless of size and propulsion, by tradition are called boats. And generally what's not a boat is a ship, unless it's a barge or some other special case. When in doubt, call it a ship.

As you continue to look at ships you will notice that some are loaded with metal boxes, some have complex crane assemblies, and others have almost nothing on deck. There are ships with bridges forward, bridges aft, and some with their bridges in the middle. The same differentiation happens with boats. Tugs become distinct from fishing boats, and ferries become a class in themselves.

But the real fun begins when the indi-vidual types of boats within each general class become recognizable. You will start to look for the subtle differences between a boat rigged for salmon and one rigged for albacore. In the ships you will begin to see that, in spite of what you first thought, not all tankers look alike. At the same time you will begin to see characteristics that indicate a vessel's age, trade, and sometimes even where it's from. With increasing knowledge of the vessels comes understanding of how they are used, their strengths and weaknesses, and a feeling for the people who sail them. It really never stops — and that's the fun of boatwatching.

Salty Talk

Abaft: Toward the stern from some point. "It's abaft the Captain's spittoon."

Aft: At, near, or toward the stern. "Go aft, young man!"

Ahoy: A salty "Hey you!"

Amidships: Near the middle of the vessel.

Avast: Stop; cease; hold; stay — reserved for extreme situations or when trying to impress lubbers.

Bar: Not what you think. A bank of sand or silt across a river or harbor. Going to sea is "crossing the bar."

Beam: Maximum width of a vessel. "She's broad in the beam."

Berth: A place to get some sack time; a place for a vessel to do likewise while lying at dock, moorings, or anchor.

Bilge: The lowest part of a vessel inside the hull. Traditionally the foulest part of the ship; hence the term "bilge rat" for a grubby sailor.

Bow: Forward end of a vessel. If a sailor is from the Eastern Atlantic, the two sides are separated and called bows.

Chart: Unlike the devices of the same name used by bureaucrats to show how taxes are spent, navigation charts are carefully-prepared maps showing water depths, land forms, hazards, bouys, lights, and other aids to navigation.

Dinghy: A small, handy boat that may be rowed or sailed and is used as a light-duty tender for another vessel; mistakenly used in reference to other crew members.

Draft: (Spelled *draught* if you say "bows.") Depth of a vessel from the waterline to the lowest point of the hull or keel.

Dredge: To remove material from the bottom of a harbor or channel; a vessel used for such removal.

Fathom: Originally, the amount of line that could be held hand to hand in outstretched arms. While some still do it that way, most modern sailors just figure a fathom is six feet.

Freeboard: Distance between main deck and the waterline.

Halyard: A line used to raise a sail.

Knot: One nautical mile per hour. Measure of speed, never used for distance. In the old days a special line called a chip log was thrown over the stern and the number of knots passing the check point in 28 seconds equaled the speed of the vessel.

Larboard: See *port.*

Lee: Sheltered side of a vessel away from the wind. All seasick people are encouraged to the lee rail.

Lubber: Salty talk for landlubber. A clumsy or unskilled seaman. Unseamanlike way of doing things.

Mile: The nautical mile is longer than the land mile, 6,080.20 feet. It is equal to one-sixtieth of a degree of latitude.

Pooping: Shipping seas over the stern; this generally happens when a vessel travels slower than following seas.

Port: (1) Sheltered place formally organized to handle cargo and passengers. (2) Opening in side of vessel — porthole, cargo port. (3) Left side of vessel looking forward (larboard on late night movies).

Quarter: The sides of a vessel near the stern.

Rig: A vessel's upper workings; her masts, sails, cargo gear, etc.

Sea Kindly: A vessel that behaves well in heavy weather in terms of pitching, rolling, and shipping water.

Sheer: Upward fore-and-aft turn of a vessel's hull or deck toward the bow and stern.

Starboard: Right side of a vessel looking forward. Originally the rudder side of a ship because the rudders were hung on the right side.

Stern: Aftermost part of a ship's hull.

Topsides: The part of a vessel's hull exposed above the waterline.

Trim: (1) The way a vessel is balanced in the water — on an even keel; down by the stern. (2) Adjusting sail position and tension to take advantage of the wind.

Tumblehome: Inward turn of a vessel's upper sides — seen most prominently on tugs.

Windward: Toward the wind. Also "weather" — the weather side.

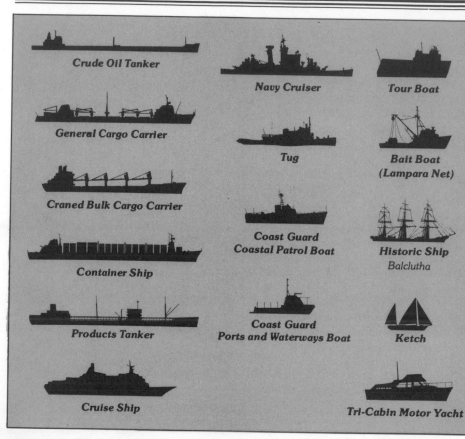

Crude Oil Tanker

General Cargo Carrier

Craned Bulk Cargo Carrier

Container Ship

Products Tanker

Cruise Ship

Navy Cruiser

Tug

Coast Guard
Coastal Patrol Boat

Coast Guard
Ports and Waterways Boat

Tour Boat

Bait Boat
(Lampara Net)

Historic Ship
Balclutha

Ketch

Tri-Cabin Motor Yacht

Note:

  Beneath most of the boat names accompanying illustrations in this book is a line of numbers separated by slanted lines. This information is an abbreviated statement of each vessel's vital statistics. The information is arranged as follows:

US/ 1972/ 70,213 dwt/ 810 ft/
Country/ Year built/ Tonnage/ Overall length/
105 ft/ 43.5 ft/ 16 kts.
Beam/ Draft/ Speed.

These symbols, found after the name of the boat, indicate the direction of the appropriate photograph.

Left ◄   Right ►   Top ▲   Bottom ▼

Merchant Shipping

At first glance, the volume of merchant shipping on San Francisco Bay appears relatively small. The occasional tankers and container ships seen passing through the Golden Gate tend to get lost in the vastness of the Bay. Inside the Golden Gate lie 450 square miles of protected waters, eight international ports, and many private docking facilities, all tied to rail, truck, air, and pipelines reaching out to the vast markets and industries of western North America. Those "occasional" ships passing beneath the bridge that connects the Bay's two peninsular breakwaters are part of a multibillion dollar industry employing hundreds of thousands.

How many ships are there? Over nine thousand each year, averaging twenty-one a day, seven days a week, every week of the year. To the delight of boat-watchers, they come and go bearing the flags of most of the maritime nations of the world. They carry oil from Alaska, Indonesia, and the Persian Gulf; molasses from Hawaii; fruit from South America; farm machinery bound for Asia; rice bound for the Orient; and cotton for the textile mills of Hong Kong and Taiwan. Tankers, car carriers, lumber barges and ships, container ships and tramp steamers pass through the portals of the Bay in all weather. Indeed, once a curious eye is cast Bayward, busy ships can be seen at the Bay's edge every minute of every day.

As such things are judged, San Francisco Bay is a relatively new port. Discovered by a Spanish overland expedition only two hundred years ago, it was infrequently used as a harbor until the 1820s. Spanish supply ships were the first international merchantmen to call at San Francisco Bay. Their holds carried European fabrics and goods from Mexico, which they traded with the colonists for tallow and animal hides. To the colonists, however, their most valuable cargo was mail, news from the outside world, and conversation with the ship's crew.

When the colony came under Mexican administration in 1820, Yankee traders from Boston became involved in the hide and tallow trade. Close in their wake came whalers and sealers, who found Richardson Bay near present-day Sausalito both a safe anchorage and a good source of water and wood for ship repairs. A settlement grew near the shore of Yerba Buena Cove, where surf lapped at what is now Montgomery Street. By 1846, when the sloop-of-war *Portsmouth* raised the American flag over the colony, it had become a respectable trade village, but hardly a port of international significance.

Two years later gold was discovered in the Sierra foothills. In the eastern United States the shout "GOLD! Gold in

California!'' brought people to shipping offices in droves. Everyone wanted to get to the goldfields and their certain fortunes by the quickest means possible. It was the age of the clipper ship, the grandest and fastest sailing vessel that ever plyed the seas. Around treacherous Cape Horn they came — the *Sea Witch, Raven, Typhoon,* and the record setting *Flying Cloud*, carrying more sail and moving faster than any ship before her. Gold seekers frightened by the Horn braved the Panamanian jungles to catch Pacific Mail's steamship *California*. In 1849 alone, merchant ships carried more than ninety-one thousand passengers and uncounted tons of cargo to San Francisco. Overnight the solitude of the vast Bay was transformed into a teeming hub of economic activity, a change from which it would never retreat.

Once in San Francisco Bay, however, the merchant fleet was one of the most unreliable in the world. They could be depended on to get both ship and cargo to San Francisco if humanly possible, but when the arduous life at sea was held up against the promise of gold, most crewmen found the return trip unattractive. Crew after crew deserted, leaving their ships to rot in the Bay's unforgiving mud. Beneath much of San Francisco's waterfront lie the buried skeletons of abandoned square-riggers. Those ships that managed to leave San Francisco often did so with less than completely volunteer crews, recruited with clubs in Barbary Coast bars.

Things have changed in the Bay's merchant fleet since those lusty days. The modern merchant ship is bigger, faster, and requires less in-port time than did her predecessors. Computers on the bridge and in the engine room and cargo spaces make her a machine well suited for a world of aerospace technology. Her long profile, capped with a button nose known as a bulbous bow, while not especially graceful, is the fastest efficient design that naval architects can provide. The old rusty three-island tramp freighters are gone, replaced by specialized ships that carry containers, drive-on ships, and a new ''freighter'' with fast-opening hydraulic hatches and heavy-duty cranes. Consistent with the modernization of the ships, the crews have become well-trained, well-paid professionals who stay with their ships voyage after voyage. Merchant shipping has become a highly competitive and costly business. Safety, cargo capacity, speed, efficiency, and dependability have become essential elements in the operation of every ship in the fleet.

The Ports of the Bay

San Francisco

In the amount of waterfront dedicated to port activities and diversity of facilities, San Francisco has the largest port on the Bay. It handles paper, automobiles, cotton, grain, liquids of various kinds, containers, passengers, and any number of other things. The Port of San Francisco has its own dredges, provides a home for San Francisco's famous fishing fleet and many of the Bay's historical ships, and serves as a hub for much of the Bay's service fleet, including the tugs, bar pilots, and water taxis. Wherever one looks, there is a bustle of international activity and a feeling that the viewer is in several different countries and ages at the same time.

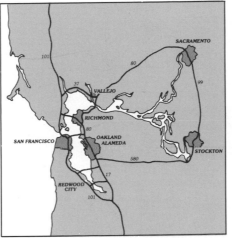

Richmond and North Bay

By tonnage, the Port of Richmond and the other port facilities along the northern edge of Contra Costa County are the monarchs of the Bay. This northern part of the Bay is tanker country. Oil and other petroleum products are the major cargos that flow through sinuous pipes to refineries and transshipment points. Sugar, molasses, bulk gypsum, and other bulk cargos are also handled in North Bay facilities.

Oakland

Across the Bay from San Francisco, the Port of Oakland is the largest containerized cargo port in the Pacific Basin, and one of the largest such facilities in the world. Its computer-coordinated yards, terminals, and cranes handle more containers laden with diverse goods than any other port in the Pacific. Oakland's terminals are also used by roll-on roll-off (Ro/Ro) ships, as well as ships carrying both containers and bulk cargo.

Sacramento, Stockton, and Redwood City

Beyond the confluence of the Sacramento and San Joaquin rivers lie the up-river ports of Sacramento and Stockton. Sacramento handles bulk grains, wood chips, and general cargo, while Stockton handles clay, coke, phosphate rock, grain, fishmeal, fertilizers, and iron ore. In the South Bay the Port of Redwood City, the maritime

Shipyards

Floating Dry Dock at Todd Shipyard

gateway to the growing Santa Clara Valley, handles primarily clay, shell, cement, and gypsum.

Alameda and Benicia

The Bay also has two privately owned and operated ports, one in Alameda across the estuary from the city of Oakland and the other at Benicia, east of San Pablo Bay on the Carquinez Strait. The Port of Benicia links the Bay to the nearby Exxon refinery, as well as being a major receiving station for automobiles manufactured in Japan. Alameda's port is the largest privately-owned open steamship terminal in the United States. It handles containerized cargo, general cargo — especially lumber and some bulk liquids.

In the early 1940s the shipyards on the Bay became virtual assembly lines for ships. War in both Europe and the Pacific meant huge movements of supplies and personnel. Ships were the only answer, and lots of them were needed quickly. At one time production was so high that the Kaiser yards at Richmond were launching a ship a day. Yards in Sausalito, San Francisco, and Alameda were also building ships, hundreds of them. But with the end of the war these hastily produced yet serviceable ships became a glut on the market. Yards either shut down or shifted over to repair and refurbishing of existing vessels.

Today the Bay's shipyards continue as repair, maintenance, and rebuilding facilities. Dry docks and graving docks are available where ships can "haul" for bottom maintenance or extensive repairs. Complete jumboizing (adding sections in the middle of the ship) and conversion capabilities offer the ship

owner a relatively inexpensive means of keeping pace with modern shipping.

Triple A Shipyard, under a lease from the Navy, operates the graving docks (a deep pit with heavy doors to close out the water) and facilities at Hunter's Point in San Francisco, making them available to merchant ships. The Port of Richmond has five additional graving docks at their main channel yards. The Bay's large floating dry docks (open structures that are sunk to receive a ship and then pumped out, lifting the ship out of the water) are operated by Todd Shipyard in Alameda and Bethlehem Steel in San Francisco. Both of the floating dry dock yards are easily viewed by the public from an appropriately safe distance.

Shipping Schedule

Each day a list of the ships arriving and departing San Francisco Bay is published in the two large daily San Francisco newspapers. Once you have learned to decipher the abbreviations used in the list, it can be a valuable aid in learning more about merchant ships. Let's use the schedule on the opposite page as an example. Suppose that after looking at the "Where to Watch Boats" section at the end of this book, you find yourself on the drawbridge over Islais Creek in San Francisco. Looking eastward you see two sparkling white States Line ships, the *Michigan* and the *Maine*. The newspaper list indicates that both are American (Am) ships powered by steam turbines (s), and that they arrived that day from Long Beach. A check of the departure schedule for the next day shows that they will be leaving for Naha, Okinawa and Yokohama, Japan respectively after one day in port.

Tuesday, May 16
ARRIVALS

VESSEL	FLAG	FROM	BERTH
Chevron Louisiana	Am. t	Estero Bay	A/9/RLW
Columbia Star	Br. m	Los Angeles	PCT-G/Oak
Esmeralda	Tr. Ves.	Chili Chili	Treasure Island
Exxon Baton Rouge	Am. t	Valdez	A/9/Benicia
Frances	Fin. m	Powell River	Pier 15/17/SF
Kamishio Maru	Ja. m	Japan	Cres/Alameda
Kashu Maru	Ja. m	Los Angeles	OOH/CT/Oak
Maine	Am. s	Long Beach	Pier 80/SF
Matsonia	Am. s	Hilo	Mat F/Oak
Michigan	Am. s	Long Beach	Pier 80/SF
Pioneer Contender	Am.P s	San Diego	OAT
Santa Maria	Am. t	Los Angeles	Unn/Rch & Olem
World Eulogy	Lib. t	San Clemente	A/9/Pac Ref.

DEPARTURES

VESSEL	FLAG	DESTINATION	BERTH
American Liberty	Am. s	Long Beach	MHT/Oak
Exxon Philadelphia	Am. t	Valdez	Triple A

Wednesday, May 17
ARRIVALS

Suecia	Sw. m	Los Angeles	RCIP
Toko Maru	Ja. m	Japan	Cres/Alameda
Veendam	Pan. m	Mazatlan	Pier 35

DEPARTURES

Maine	Am. s	Yokohama	Pier 80/SF
Marine Chemist	Am. t	US Gulf	Martinez
Michigan	Am. s	Naha	Pier 92/SF

Shipping Schedule reprinted courtesy of *San Francisco Examiner.*

Shipping Schedule Abbreviations

t: Tanker
m: Motorship (Diesel powered)
s: Steamship
A/9: Anchorage 9
Cres/Alameda: Encinal Terminals, Alameda
Mat: Matson Navigation Company Terminal
MHT: Oakland Middle Harbor Terminal
OAT: Oakland Army Terminal
OOH: Oakland Outer Harbor Terminal
Pac.Ref.: Pacific Refinery, Hercules
PCT: Public Container Terminal, Oakland
RCIP: Richmond Canal Industrial Park
RLW: Richmond Long Wharf
Triple A: Triple A Shipyard, Hunters Point
Unn/Rch & Oleum: Union Oil, Richmond & Oleum

Beyond the States Line ships, three tankers lie at anchor in the Bay. Checking the list again, you see that three tankers (t) are listed as going to Anchorage 9 (A/9). Two are American-registered and the third is Liberian. "Valdez" in the "from" column beside the *Exxon Baton Rouge* indicates that it is carrying crude oil loaded at the southern end of the Trans-Alaska pipeline. While in Anchorage 9 the *Exxon Baton Rouge* will unload some of its cargo to a barge, or "lighter off," to reduce its draft for the trip to Benicia.

Used by the many people interested in marine shipping, the list is derived from information supplied by the Marine Exchange, and is a small sample of their "marine intelligence" system.

Hull Design

At sea, the two things that have the largest influence on a merchant ship's efficiency are the power plant and the form of her hull. The power plant limits how much power can be delivered by the ship's screws to push her through the water, while the shape of the hull determines the amount of resistance the water will offer to the ship's movement. Since the bow is the first part of the hull to meet the water, its shape is critical to how a vessel passes through the water. In faster ships the so-called "wave-making resistance" of the bow may account for as much as half of the total water resistance. Slower vessels have less wave-making resistance, so the bow can be fuller like those seen on barges. But the bow of a modern fast merchant ship must be as slender as strength and cargo capacity will allow.

Plumb bows were common on ships built in the early part of this century. They had very little flair and tended to slice through rather than rise to oncoming waves, which meant that their foredecks were often awash with green water.

Clipper bows closely resemble those seen on the majestic sailing ships of the late nineteenth century. They have a pronounced flair that deflects waves and spray, making for dryer foredecks, and they are most common in modern passenger liners.

Raked bows, while they have less flair than clipper bows, tend to ride over oncoming waves and have smaller bow waves and thus less wave-making resistance. This is the most common bow form on modern merchant ships.

Spoon or cutter bows are essentially raked bows with a convex shape. Once common, they are now seen only on a few older merchants still in service.

Maierform bows look much like spoon bows when the ship is in the water. Below the waterline, however, the stem has a pronounced increase in the rake to the keel. In theory this form is more streamlined and reduces pitching. It is mainly seen on Scandinavian ships.

Bulbous bows are a strange yet effective innovation of modern ship design. They are raked from the forepeak to the waterline, then turn forward to form a large, round bulb. The effect of the bulb is to significantly reduce the bow wave and pitching, allowing the ship to go faster without increasing the horsepower.

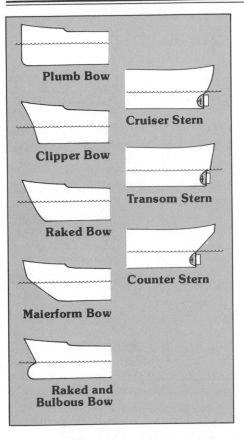

Plumb Bow

Clipper Bow

Raked Bow

Maierform Bow

Raked and Bulbous Bow

Cruiser Stern

Transom Stern

Counter Stern

The shape of a ship's stern influences the speed of the ship through its effect on the length of the waterline and the effectiveness of the ship's propellers. The longer the waterline, or wetted surface, of a vessel the faster it can move through the water, other things being equal. Designers try to increase the wetted stern length, but must balance length against its effect on the ship's stern wake and the effectiveness of the propellers. If water flows smoothly by the stern and through the propellers, they can deliver maximum thrust without vibration and power loss.

The merchant cruiser stern is the most common form seen in today's merchant ships. Its spoon-shaped profile increases the waterline length when loaded, while maximizing the effective thrust of the propeller. Generally a merchant cruiser stern indicates a single-screwed vessel.

The cruiser stern resembles the stern frequently used on naval cruisers. It is seldom used on American merchant ships, and is generally seen only on multiple-screwed ships.

The transom stern, except in the most modern merchant ships, is also a multiple-screw form. It offers a very long waterline for speed, and its flat underwater profile tends to reduce squatting at high speeds. It is common in fast naval ships, Coast Guard cutters, and newer merchants. Many of the container, LASH, and roll-on/roll-off (Ro/Ro) ships built in the seventies are single-screwed variations on the transom theme.

Counter sterns are rare today, but were common in the merchant ships of the early 1900s. The distinguishing feature of the counter stern is the sharp knuckle midway in the stern line, which reduced pooping by following seas.

19

Engines

By the time San Francisco Bay became a major port, machines were replacing wind as the prime mover of ships. Pacific Mail Steamship Company's *California*, a wooden-hulled side-wheeler, chugged and splashed through the Gate in 1849 with a load of gold-hungry passengers from Panama. The *California* was followed by other ocean-going side-wheelers, but their heyday was destined to be short. In 1874 Pacific Mail built an iron-hulled, propeller-driven steamer that was both faster and stronger. Shortly after World War I the piston-driven steam engine itself was superseded by the more efficient turbine.

Today, merchant ships are powered by several different kinds of engines. The oil-fired boiler/steam turbine is used by many ship builders, but it is not their exclusive choice. Diesel engines, sometimes as tall as a four-story building, have become common, and gas turbines are proving increasingly practical. There have also been experiments with nuclear power, but the atom has, so far, been an unacceptably costly fuel, and the power plants are too expensive to build, too.

Today's **steam turbine**, while large, is a relatively simple means of propelling larger ships. The oil-fired boiler is basically a fire box with water tubes running through it. The heat of the burning oil converts fresh water to super-heated steam which is then injected, under pressure, into the turbine. Inside the turbine, the steam passes through a series of many bladed rotors that are attached to a central shaft, like wind blowing through a series of windmill rotors. The expanding steam causes the rotors to spin rapidly, in fact too fast for the ship's propeller. Reduction gears change the speed from several thousand revolutions per minute at the turbine to one hundred or so RPM at the propeller.

The steam turbine is both efficient and quiet. However, it has one major disadvantage. The boilers must be constantly fired, both underway and in port. This is the most common form of power in all of the types of merchant ships seen on the Bay, as well as in the majority of military ships. Steam turbine powered ships are called *steamships* (SS).

The **diesel motors** used in ships are the same as those used in trucks and tractors, but larger and slower-turning. They are similar to automobile engines in that fuel is mixed with air, and then fed into a cylinder where it burns. The burning mixture expands, forcing the piston down, which in turn rotates the crank shaft. No spark plugs are used in diesel motors. Instead the fuel mixture is ignited by the upward compression of the piston. The pistons in ship diesels are sometimes several feet across, with cylinders large enough for an engineer to stand inside. Slow-turning diesels run at 100 RPM and medium speed diesels at 150 to 450 RPM.

Diesels are more fuel-efficient than steam turbines, and they don't have to run in port, but they are considerably heavier than a turbine of the same horse-power. Due to rising fuel costs, diesels are becoming increasingly common, especially in the tramp trade and on some tankers. Diesel ships are called *motorships* (MS).

The **gas turbine** has been used in some fast military ships and smaller spe-cialty vessels, including the Golden Gate Ferries, but is only beginning to make significant inroads into the merchant fleet. The operating principle is basically the same as that of the steam turbine, except that hot gas is used in place of steam. The power from the turbine may drive the ship directly in a water-jet sys-tem, through reduction gears or through

an electric generator and motor system like that used in some Chevron tankers. Ships with this type of engine are called *gas turbine ships* (GTS).

There are only a handful of operating **nuclear-powered** merchant ships in the world today. Rising costs of petro-leum fuels may, however, make nuclear merchant ships economically practical in the future. Essentially, a nuclear ship uses a conventional steam turbine with an atomic reactor rather than an oil-fired boiler. There is no exhaust, and the reactor doesn't consume air, which is what makes nuclear power practical for submarines. Ships powered by nuclear reactors are called *nuclear ships* (NS).

Electric motor drive is not common in merchant ships. Power is supplied to an electric generator by either a steam turbine or a diesel engine. The electricity produced by the generator turns an

electric motor that is connected to the ship's propeller. Electric drive systems are very reliable, require relatively little maintenance, and are very quiet. Most nonnuclear submarines have electric drive. Electrically-powered ships are designated either *diesel electric ships* (DES) or *turbine electric ships* (TES).

Propellers

The first mechanically-powered mer-chant ships were side-wheelers that looked like clipper ships with water wheels stuck on the sides. Sails were re-tained to supplement the steam-driven wheel in favorable winds, making the ships look like they were not quite sure what they were supposed to be. As ships grew larger and their steam engines more powerful, both the sails and the side-wheel were replaced by a more effi-

21

cient propeller, which delivered backward thrust as it spun in the water. Since then other methods of power delivery have been developed, but the propeller has remained the dominant method in merchant shipping.

In recent years there has been a trend away from multiple propellers, which were once thought essential to maneuvering large ships. Now most merchant ships have a single "screw." Most single screws are "variable pitch," which means that the individual blades can be rotated on their axes to change how the propeller cuts through the water. With this type of propeller, a ship can take a greater bite of the water when starting and reduce the bite once cruising speed is achieved for maximum fuel economy. In addition, the variable-pitch propeller allows the ship to be backed without changing the direction of the propeller's rotation.

Bow thrusters are another modern development of propeller use that has become common in larger ships. The bow thruster is a reversible propeller located in an athwartships tube well forward in the bow below the waterline. Water is pushed from one side to the other through the thruster, causing the bow to move in the opposite direction. The use of bow thrusters has greatly reduced the need for tugs and speeded the docking process.

Tonnage and Displacement

There are five different ways to answer the question, "How many tons is that ship?" All of these answers are correct, yet none is equivalent to the others. Because of this confusion, it's important to know which figure is being used when tonnage is discussed.

Gross and **net tonnage** are figures used to express the capacity of a ship rather than her weight. The ton in this case is equal to 100 cubic feet (or 2.83 cubic meters). These figures are established and registered according to international convention, and serve as the basis for port charges and chartering fees. **Gross registered tonnage** is the total capacity of all the ship's spaces below and above decks. **Net registered tonnage** is the amount of earning space available, and is determined by deducting the volume of working spaces (engine room, ballast, fuel tanks, etc.) and crew quarters from the gross tonnage.

Deadweight tonnage is another commonly-encountered figure. In this case tonnage is actually a measure of the ship's weight, or displacement. Ships are rarely weighed directly. Instead, their weight is determined by measuring how much water is displaced when the ship is floated. Knowing how much the water weighs, it becomes a simple matter to

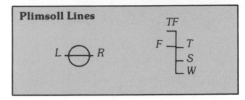

Plimsoll Lines

compute the "displacement" of the ship. Three displacement figures are used. **Light displacement** is the weight of the vessel's hull, engine, spare parts, and other operating equipment. **Load displacement** is the vessel's weight when fully loaded including crew, cargo, passengers, fuel, and ballast. International law requires that the load displacement be indicated on the ship's side by Plimsoll Lines (see Ship's Markings). **Deadweight tonnage** is the difference between the light and load displacements. Note that deadweight is not the same as net tonnage because deadweight includes things like fuel, ballast, and fresh water, which are not part of the ship's earning capacity.

Ship's Markings

Aside from the name that appears on both bows and the stern of a ship, there are several hull markings that are of interest. On each side of both the bows and stern will be a series of numbers ascending toward the main deck. These numbers show the ship's *draft* — how much of it is below the waterline. On American, British, and many other ships, the numbers indicate feet. On other ships, particularly those from Scandinavian countries, the numbers indicate the ship's draft in meters.

Merchant ship hulls are generally two colors. The part of the hull normally below the water when the ship is loaded is painted with red "antifouling" paint to prevent marine organisms from growing on the hull, which would slow the ship down. Above, the hull may be any color. Amidships, near the top of the bottom paint, is a vertical line with several lines coming out of it parallel to the waterline. This marking is called the Plimsoll Line, after the British civil servant who created it to prevent overloading, which en-

dangered seamen's lives. The parallel lines indicate the maximum load displacement in waters of varying density. Beside the Plimsoll Line is a circle with a horizontal line through it, which indicates the registered displacement tonnage of the ship. The letters on the line indicate the registering agency. LR, for example, indicates Lloyds Register, by far the most common for ships seen on the Bay.

The most prominent markings on most ships are the company symbols painted on the stacks and sometimes repeated on the point of the bow. Frequently, however, the operating company has chartered the ship. Someone else owns it. The ship's owner determines the country of registration, making it possible for ships with the same stack patterns to be registered in several different countries.

Liquid Cargo Carriers

Gold, yellow gold, first made San Francisco Bay a major international port. Today gold is still the major interest of the Bay's merchant fleet, but the color has changed. With more than eight hundred miles of sheltered shoreline, access to shore transportation, and suitable refinery sites, San Francisco Bay is an ideal place to receive and refine oil, black gold, that increasingly precious commodity of international commerce.

At first the ubiquitousness of the tankers is not apparent. Standard Oil's Richmond long wharf is the only place where the public can easily see tankers alongside a pier. The other tankers are seen only in transit, or occasionally lying at anchor in Anchorage 9, lightening their load or waiting for a berth to open. But appearances to the contrary, ton for cargo ton, dollar for cargo dollar, and ship for ship, tankers are the dominant ships in the Bay's merchant fleet.

Most of the tankers carry oil to the refineries along San Pablo Bay and the Carquinez Strait. The tanker piers rest at the edge of the shipping channel, sometimes a mile or more from land, looking more like afterthoughts than places to tie up ocean vessels. Narrow causeway roads overtop several large pipes, and together they connect the piers to tank farms sprouting on the adjacent hills.

Corn syrup, animal fat, and molasses are also significant cargos, although considerably less in volume than petroleum products. Molasses is part of the San Francisco Hawaii sugar trade, and molasses tankers discharge at the C&H plant in Crockett or the molasses terminal at Point San Pablo. In addition to having been the last active whaling station in the United States, Point San Pablo is one of the animal fat terminals on the Bay. Animal fat also flows from San Francisco's Islais Creek terminal and the bulk liquid terminal in Alameda.

Think of trying to carry a lidless, full can of paint up a shaky ladder. Moving liquids from one place to another can be challenging. Tankers, of course, have lids, but the challenge of carrying sloshing liquids is still great. The sloshing effect is reduced by compartmentalizing the ship's hold with a few longitudinal and several transverse bulkheads, or walls. In addition, the extreme forward and after bulkheads are reinforced double walls called *cofferdams*. The cofferdams isolate the tank section of the ship from other spaces, thus reducing fire hazard when the tanker is carrying flammable cargo.

Tanker cargo is loaded through amidships manifolds, then passes through pipes along the midline to the various tanks. A railed catwalk over the pipes enables the crew to move fore and aft safely when the decks are awash. Pumps and heaters driven by steam from the

Supertankers

ship's boilers make it possible for most tankers to discharge their cargo in all weather.

Lacking the cranes and other deck gear associated with dry cargo, the tanker has a very distinctive, uncluttered profile. Near the forward end of the ship there is always a single mast. This mast is fitted with a bright white light, which marks the forward end of the tanker at night. Occasionally the forward mast is also fitted with a crow's-nest for the bow watch.

"Three-island" tankers, with the navigation bridge and the engine amidships, are becoming less common because they have less cargo space for the same length of ship, but they are still seen frequently on the Bay. Far more common are tankers with the bridge and engine in the stern, leaving the full length of the ship forward of the bridge, save the forecastle, for cargo. The forecastle stores anchor chain and mooring gear.

While it's unlikely that supertankers will ever be seen on San Francisco Bay, no discussion of tankers would be complete without some mention of the Very Large Crude-oil Carriers (VLCCs) now frequenting the oceans of the world. The Bay, large as it is, is a good example of why these monsters are seldom seen anywhere but in the news. Outside the Golden Gate lies an extensive crescent-shaped sand bar that makes dredging necessary just to maintain a shipping channel 50 feet deep. Also, most of the berths on the Bay are 40 feet deep or less. The VLCCs seldom draw less than 60 feet, and some go as deep as 93 feet.

The VLCCs are simply too big to fit into most of the world's ports. With rare exceptions, to get their cargo to refineries they must "lighter off," discharging their cargo to smaller tankers in the deeper offshore waters. In some cases they can approach the shore closely enough to use floating lines. Their size also creates serious maintenance problems because there are so few dry docks large enough to pull them out of the water. Sea routes are also limited for VLCCs because neither the Panama nor the Suez canal can accommodate super tankers, and several of the channels between islands that are taken for granted by other ships are too shallow for VLCCs.

How big are they? Imagine two parallel lines of four end-to-end football fields with the whole thing standing as tall as an eight-story building. There is so much inertia in its 400,000 deadweight tons that turning or stopping must be done with extreme care. If one of these giants merely bumped a pier, there wouldn't be anything left of the pier to rebuild. In spite of their size, or because of it, they are single screwed, and are driven at 16 knots by steam turbines.

SS *Chevron California* ▶

US/ 1972/ 70,213 dwt/ 810 ft /
Country/ Year built/ Tonnage/ Overall length/
105 ft/ 43.5 ft
Beam/ Draft/ Speed

This seagull's-eye view of the *Chevron California* gives some idea of the massiveness of Bay tankers. The pipes connecting her eighteen cargo tanks can be seen along the ship's midline. The transverse piping amidships leads to the loading/unloading manifolds. The masts and booms just inboard of the manifolds are for handling the hoses that link the ship to oil pipes ashore. The *Chevron California* is a medium tanker among those seen on the Bay. The largest tankers may reach 120,000 deadweight tons.

(Photo courtesy Chevron Shipping Company)

GTT *Chevron Oregon* ▶

US/ 1975/ 39,789 dwt/ 651 ft/
96 ft/ 38 ft/ 1 screw

Chevron's gas turboelectric tankers are easily distinguished by their square "funnels." Their single gas turbine powered electric motor delivers 12,500 Shaft Horsepower (SHP) to a single controllable-pitch propeller. The *Chevron Oregon* and her sister ships are crude oil carriers connecting the Richmond Standard Oil refinery with the pipeline terminal in Valdez, Alaska. They have a spoon rather than a bulbous bow, and are equipped with a bow thruster.

(Photo courtesy Chevron Shipping Company)

SS *Exxon Newark* ▼

US/ 1952/ 17,378 gt/ 628 ft/
82.7 ft/ 33.5 ft/ 16kts

This is a classic tanker. Its raised
forecastle, amidships bridge, and after
superstructure are the "three-island"
design common in older tankers. She
is small by modern standards, with
approximately one-eighth the capacity
of the offshore Very Large Crude Carriers.
In spite of this the *Exxon Newark* is
a medium-sized tanker among those
seen on the Bay. The bulbous bow, visible
because the ship is "light," was added
after she was built.

SS *Manhattan* ▲

US/ 1962/ 62,434 gt/ 1011 ft/
133 ft/ 53 ft/ 17.5 kts

The *Manhattan* was originally built as an icebreaker/tanker in an attempt to bring Alaska's North Slope oil to the East Coast via the Arctic Ocean. One successful trip was made, but the experiment demonstrated that Arctic Ocean shipping was both costly and impractical. For a short time after her Arctic experience the *Manhattan* was used as a bulk grain carrier. But now she is back in the Alaska black oil trade, carrying crude oil from the end of the pipeline in Valdez, Alaska to the Exxon refinery in Benicia and to other California ports. Her unique bow profile may frequently be seen at Anchorage 9.

MV *Exxon Galveston* ▶

*US/1970 Conv. 1978/27,248 dwt/552.5 ft/
95 ft/29.5 ft/7,200 hp/12 kts*

The *Exxon Galveston* is one of the
more unusual tankers seen on the Bay.
Originally she was an integrated tug and
barge, operating on the East Coast.
When she was converted, the tug's
engines were installed in the barge and
the bridge was added. Presently the
Galveston is being used to lighter other
Exxon tankers at Anchorage 9 so they
can make the trip through the Carquinez
Strait to Exxon's Benicia terminal.

MV *Stolt Sincerity* ◀

*Liberia/1956/18,570 gt/580 ft/
88.5 ft/38 ft*

The name *Stolt* on the side of a Bay
tanker identifies the ship as a "chemical
tanker." Superficially they look like oil
tankers, but closer examination reveals a
complicated system of deck-borne pipes
that are different from those seen on an
oil tanker. Chemical tankers may carry
animal, vegetable, and marine fats, lube
oil, solvents, acids, and other chemicals.
Often they carry several different chemicals at once.

29

General Purpose Cargo Ships

Manuel Mejia ▶
*Colombia/ 1957/ 5,250 gt/ 475 ft/
62 ft/ 23.5 ft/ 17 kts*

While the old three-island freighter has been almost completely replaced by modern, more efficient ships, the general purpose carrier still performs a vital function in world shipping. Ship owners find them profitable enough to build new ones with heavy steel cargo cranes and derricks, hydraulically-operated folding steel hatches, and economical diesel engines. The superstructure and engines have been moved three-quarters or full aft to increase cargo capacity, and the equipment has been automated, where practical, to minimize crew requirements and to speed cargo handling. General cargo ships are called either *liners* or *tramps*, depending on the way their services are used.

Liners sail between designated ports on established schedules, and may carry several hundred different lots of cargo. Their cargos are generally palletized (loaded on wooden pallets that can be moved about by fork lifts), break-bulk (loose cargo such as cotton bales, oil drums, or rolls of newsprint), bag-bulk (bagged cargo such as coffee, alfalfa pellets, or fertilizer), or a combination of the three. Liners can also handle occasional heavy loads such as farm machinery or locomotives. Liners can carry up to twelve passengers without being classified as passenger vessels.

Today's **tramps**, while they retain the title, are a far cry from the inefficient tramp steamers of the late night movies. Unlike liners, tramps sail when and where cargo is available, frequently with a shipload of a single cargo such as grain or scrap steel. Their cargos are generally loaded in bulk, and are of a lower value than those carried by liners. Although liners may be designed to carry specific cargos on the routes they serve, tramps are designed for general service and never carry passengers.

The *Manuel Mejia* is typical of general service cargo liners. Designed primarily to handle break-bulk cargos, she can also handle refrigerated and containerized cargo. She is fitted with standard cargo cranes, and her superstructure is three-quarters aft. The *Manuel Mejia* is operated by Grancolombiana between the western ports of North America and the Pacific ports of Central and South America.

MV *Nordpol* ▼

*Denmark/ 1974/ 19,589 gt/ 587 ft/
88.7 ft/ 40 ft/ 15 kts*

Modern in every way, *Nordpol* is proof that there are still profits in the tramp trade. Seen here delivering containers, she is an example of the versatility built into modern bulk carriers. Most new container ships are faster, but when speed is not critical the bulk carrier will get cargo to its destination cheaper. The best indications of *Nordpol's* recent vintage are the simple versatility of her cargo cranes and her full aft superstructure.

Container Ships

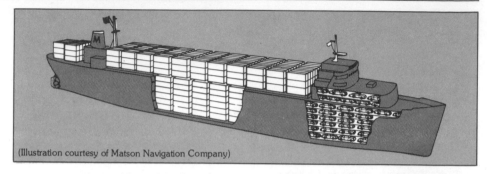

(Illustration courtesy of Matson Navigation Company)

The revolution worked by the introduction of the standard container in the shipping industry is the equivalent of the horse being replaced by Mr. Ford's motorcar. Now cargos once handled by many people representing several companies can be loaded at the factory into standard containers. The cargo is placed in the container by the people who know the needs of that particular cargo best, then the container is hauled by truck or train to a port terminal, where huge cranes place it on a ship. When the ship arrives at its destination, the process is reversed.

Like the very large tankers, container ships have grown and are continuing to grow. Many are now over 900 feet long and carry up to two thousand containers. In the fully cellular container ship, the containers are stacked on top of each other in vertical rails. The bigger ships can carry containers six deep and ten wide inside the ship, with another three layers on deck. Most container ships are powered by large steam turbines and are single screwed. Most of the larger container ships depend on shoreside cranes, but several of the newer ships have large gantry cranes that allow them to be independent of shore facilities other than trucks to haul the containers away.

(Photo Courtesy Matson Navigation Company)

SS *Hawaiian Enterprise* ▼▲
US/ 1970/ 38,800 dt/ 720 ft/ 95 ft/ 50 ft/ 23 kts

While the *Hawaiian Enterprise* and her sister ship the *Hawaiian Progress* look like fully containerized ships, they can also carry 135,000 cubic feet of general cargo and 5,000 long tons of molasses, a commodity that Matson ships have carried from the Hawaiian Islands since the line was first established in the days of the square-riggers. The cargo space is often filled with automobiles, which are difficult to get back and forth from the Islands by any other means.

SS *President McKinley* ▲

US/ 1968/ 17,801 gt/ 664 ft/ 82 ft/ 30.5 ft

Half of the container ship story is the giant shoreside gantry cranes required to handle the containers. In this photograph the *President McKinley* is being loaded at her Oakland Middle Harbor terminal. The crane operator rides 200 feet above the ground in the moving car visible in the center of the picture. With this kind of crane the *President McKinley* can be completely unloaded and reloaded in less than twenty-four hours.

33

Roll-on/Roll-off Ships

SS Maine ▼

US/ 1975/ 33,765 dt/ 684 ft/ 102 ft/ 32 ft/ 23 kts

The Ro/Ros offer many of the in-port speed advantages of container ships without the disadvantage of the cargo having to fit into a standard container. Anything that can be driven on the road can be driven onto a Ro/Ro, either by a stern-mounted driveway or bridges that mount on side cargo ports. Ro/Ros generally have single screws powered by steam turbines. In addition, many have bow thrusters to aid in the docking process.

The two cranes on the forward part of the ship allow her to load general cargo into her single hold, deck-load containers, and lift heavy objects up to 30 tons. The stern ramp can accept loads up to 65 tons. She gains maneuverability with a 1,500 horsepower bow thruster.

Similar ships are operated by Pacific Australia Direct Line (PAD) out of Oakland's Seventh Street Terminal.

(Illustration courtesy of States Line)

(Photo courtesy Matson Navigation Company)

SS *Lurline* ◄

US/ 1973/ 25,350 dt/ 300 ft/
105 ft/ 28 ft/ 24 kts

The *Lurline* and *Matsonia* are "trailership" Ro/Ros operated by Matson Navigation Company out of their container terminal in Oakland's Outer Harbor. Cargo is driven aboard in standard truck trailers via three shoreside bridges, which mount on the side of the ship. The need for these bridges limits their ports of call to Los Angeles, Honolulu, and Oakland. Like other Matson ships, in addition to general cargo, the trailerships carry molasses and automobiles.

Dry Cargo Carriers

Once there were only a few basic kinds of merchant ships; tankers, passenger liners, bulk carriers, and all-purpose freighters. There were differences among the various freighters, but they were subtle. They all had four or five cargo holds. Their navigation bridge, crew accommodations, and machinery spaces were amidships, and masts with sturdy wooden booms stood ready to hoist cargo in and out of the holds. Both the forecastle and the poop deck over the stern were raised above the main deck giving them a characteristic "three-island" profile. The old freighters could carry anything short of heavy cargo like locomotives and bulk ore; sometimes they even carried those.

The old freighters had one major disadvantage, however, other than the fact that they were slow. They spent as much time in port as they did underway.

Loading and unloading freighter cargo was labor intensive and time consuming. Port costs continued to escalate to the point that it was less expensive to operate a ship between ports than it was when she was beside a pier. Ship builders redesigned the cargo crane and hatches, but that was not enough. Then, in 1956, Sea Land Service introduced an entirely new concept in shipboard cargo handling, the container. Looking like truck trailer bodies, containers could be hauled by both trucks and trains, as well as stacking neatly aboard ships. Individual containers could be loaded at the point of origin and unloaded at the cargo's ultimate destination, minimizing shipping hazards, handling, and time. In port, the turn-around time was shortened from two weeks for conventional cargo to one or two days for containers.

Container ships now dominate all of the major world trade routes, but not completely. There are still many cargos and ports for which containerization is not the answer. Bulk paper, automobiles, lumber, and many other things simply don't fit into containers very well. Small ports with little activity can't afford the shore development associated with containerized cargo. To meet these needs, hybrid ships have been built that are part conventional cargo carriers and part container ships. Specialty ships have also been built that carry cars, lumber, or other cargos with unique needs. Finally, the remaining strength of the freighter, its ability to handle diverse cargos without specialized shore facilities, has been challenged by another innovation, the roll-on/roll-off (Ro/Ro) ship. Ro/Ros can carry anything that can travel on a road, and are loaded via driveways rather than by slow cargo cranes.

Hybrid Ships

The broad acceptance of the container in the world's ports has caused many ship owners to build combination carriers or to convert some of their conventional ships to carry both containers and general cargo. These ships may call at ports without shoreside container cranes, so they must have their own deck gear to load and unload containers. Because these carriers are expensive to build, they are generally used only as liners. The presence of heavy-duty cargo cranes makes the hybrid ships easy to distinguish from cellular container ships, but they can be confused with the conventional cargo carrier when in ballast (unloaded). The hybrid ships may be powered by either diesel engines or steam turbines, but generally are single screwed.

SS Idaho

US/ 1969/ 13,074 dwt/ 579 ft/ 82 ft/ 31 ft/ 24,000 SHP/ 23 kts

The *Idaho* is a good example of the versatility built into the modern general cargo carrier. Heavy lift cranes over holds three and four, as well as wide hatches, allow rapid handling of both bulk and containerized cargo. The *Idaho* can carry 118 containers below and 132 containers on deck. The *Idaho* and her sister ships *Colorado, Montana, Wyoming,* and *Michigan* operate out of Pier 80 in San Francisco.

Specialized Carriers

Imagine how many newspapers are printed in the Bay Area, California, or the West each day. Millions of tons of newsprint are consumed in the act of keeping the public informed about the events and products of the day. Where does all that paper come from? The answer, of course, is trees; but the trees in this case, as well as the paper mills, are in British Columbia. Newsprint is a heavy cargo and the demand for it is too great to make shipping by truck or train practical. Newsprint is also a relatively fragile cargo. The combination of its fragility and its large, sustained market has justified building ships with specially-designed holds and cranes for handling the huge rolls of newsprint.

The market for European and Japanese cars is also large and sustained. In fact, the market is so large that ships resembling oddly-shaped boxes are seen on the Bay almost every day. Steel plating reaches well above the main deck

without even a hint of a porthole, and the name of an automobile company is often emblazoned on their sides. Inside these strange vessels, up to ten decks are interconnected by internal ramps. These decks carry as many as three thousand consumers of tanker-carried oil. Side hatches facilitate driving the cars on and off the ship. Sometimes these ships are filled with containers for their return trip to help defray the cost of operating the ship.

Lumber, paper pulp, bananas, and many other cargos are also carried by specialty ships which can frequently be seen on the Bay.

Friendship ▲

Liberia/ 1976/ 6,101 gt/ 574.5 ft/ 84 ft/ 26.6 ft/ 13,100 hp/ 18 kts

The car carriers are easily the strangest-looking ships on the Bay and, by virtue of their shoe-box shape, the most easily recognized. Inside the box, multiple decks are interconnected by ramps making fast drive-on/drive-off loading and unloading possible. The *Friendship* uses stern ramps to get her automobile cargo to the pier, while some of the other car carriers use side cargo ports. Car carriers may be seen in Richmond, Benicia, Alameda, and at Pier 70 in San Francisco.

MV *Universal Wing* ▶

*Panama/ 1976/ 20,705 gt/ 593 ft/
—/ 39 ft/ 14,000 hp/ 15 kts*

With the name emblazoned on her side it's hard to mistake the *Universal Wing's* trade, but from a distance she looks like many of the modern bulk carriers seen on the Bay. She is designed to handle automobiles either with her fast cargo cranes or through side cargo ports. She is seen here at the Pasha Terminal at the foot of Canal Boulevard in Richmond.

MV *Queensland* ◀

*Sweden/ 1970/ 22,759 gt/ 656 ft/
89 ft/ 36.5 ft/ 16 kts*

The *Queensland* is a specialized bulk carrier. Though her hull has been strengthened to handle ore cargo, her cranes and deck rails indicate that her primary trade is lumber. Lumber is a major cargo in Western Pacific trade routes, and ships like *Queensland* run regularly between British Columbia and Europe. On the return trip from Europe she may carry ore part of the way to minimize costs.

39

Passenger Ships

Before the introduction of jet air travel in the late 1950s, the only practical means a businessman had to get to his Pacific Basin customers was the passenger liner. Hawaii, Hong Kong, Tokyo, and Sydney were all connected to the Bay Area by the "grand ladies of the sea," which made regular trips back and forth. Enroute the travelers had several different "classes" of travel to choose from. In first class no expense was spared in trying to duplicate the accommodations — food, service, and living space alike — that one would find in a fine hotel. Cabin and tourist classes offered more modest accommodations at reduced prices. It was an expensive way to make a business trip and it was slow, but few could argue with the relaxation a sea cruise offered.

Until recently, most steamship passengers traveled on "liners," ships that traveled established routes between designated ports according to regular schedules. The vacation traveler went to established commercial ports or waited for space aboard the few available cruise ships. Today, as a glance at the travel section of any newspaper will show, there has been a dramatic shift. The cruise ships going to exotic places like Alaska's Inland Passage, Puerto Vallarta, Papeete, or the Galapagos Islands are now the carriers of the passenger ship tradition. Most of the giants of the North Atlantic trade that carried two thousand passengers at 35 knots are gone. Today's sleek diesel or steam turbine powered cruise ships, carrying five hundred to nine hundred passengers at less than 25 knots, are more interested in passenger comfort than in speed. Recreation programs, lectures, and big-name entertainment supplement the excellent food and comfortable accommodations.

In addition to the cruise ships, passengers are also carried by many cargo liners. The passenger/cargo liner, as the name implies, is designed to carry both passengers and cargo. It can carry up to a hundred fare-paying people, and has many of the amenities found on the all-passenger cruise ships. The cargo liner, on the other hand, can carry only twelve passengers, and the accommodations are limited by the fact that the ship is designed primarily to carry cargo. The fares on the cargo liners are generally equivalent to tourist class fares on passenger ships, and the quality of the accommodations varies from ship to ship. Sometimes the passenger spaces on cargo liners rival those on cruise ships, while giving passengers the advantages of informality and close association with the ship's crew.

(Photo courtesy Royal Viking Line)

MS *Royal Viking Star*

*No/ 1971/ 21,500 gt/ 580 ft/
82.6 ft/ —/ 21 kts*

Royal Viking Lines operates the *Royal Viking Star* and two sister ships between the Caribbean, Panama, Latin America, Florida, and the West Coast. Their Bay Area berth is Pier 35 in San Francisco. They are one-class ships; services to all passengers are the same, with the fares based on the size of the living accommodations. They are twin screwed and diesel powered.

SS *Santa Mercedes*

US/ 1962/ 11,221 gt/ 547 ft/ 79 ft/ 29 ft/ 20 kts

Delta Lines operates this and three sister ships out of Piers 30 and 32 in San Francisco. Its passenger space includes staterooms for a hundred people, club, lounge, dining room, and swimming pool. Deck gear includes gantry cranes for containers and derricks for bulk cargo. Gyrostabilizer fins help smooth its passage through the water, and a 19,800 SHP steam turbine turns its single screw.

Navy

When the sloop-of-war *Portsmouth* and a thrown-together "fleet" of chartered merchant ships officially raised the American flag over San Francisco Bay in 1846, there was very little to indicate that it would soon become the busiest harbor on the Pacific. San Francisco was a sleepy village on the shore of Yerba Buena Cove. There were no piers because there wasn't a need for them. Ships visited the Bay only occasionally. But the military men recognized that the Bay was more than a beautiful, safe harbor. They saw the expanse of the Bay as a strategically important base for the American Navy on the great Pacific Ocean.

Gold changed the look of the Bay, but not the understanding of the Navy. Today, with over six hundred ship visits annually, their early vision proves itself daily.

Naval Ship Designations and Names

All U.S. Navy ships are assigned designations that indicate their type and general use. The first letters indicate the general class of the ship:

A - Auxiliary ships used to support combat ships
C - Aircraft carriers
D - Destroyers
F - Frigates
L - Amphibious warfare ships
M - Mine warfare vessels
P - Patrol boats
SS - Submarines
T - Military Sealift Command ships
Y - Yard service craft

Subsequent letters indicate the specific type of ship within each general class. If the letter "N" appears at the end of the designation, the ship is powered by nuclear reactors. The letter "G" at the end indicates that the ship is capable of firing guided missiles.

The Navy currently has 175 different types of ships in its active fleet. Most of the more specialized types, however, are rarely if ever seen on the Bay.

Ship names may also be used as a guide to the ship's type, since ship names are selected according to traditions for each of the types. As the Navy's ships have been modernized, and new ship types have appeared, however, the ship-naming traditions have been adjusted. As a result, ship names alone may be confusing. Without its SSBN designator, the *Patrick Henry* could be either a destroyer or a fleet ballistic missile submarine. If you read the name *Long Beach* in a newspaper you might not know that it's a nuclear guided missile cruiser rather than a fast combat support ship, attack nuclear submarine, or amphibious cargo ship, all of which have been or are named after cities.

The following list of type designators and current naming procedures is for the Navy ships most likely to be seen on San Francisco Bay. For a more complete discussion of U.S. Navy ships, see *Jane's Fighting Ships*, an exhaustive encyclopedia that is available at most public libraries.

AD - Destroyer tender (named after regions of significance, particularly National Parks; USS *Bryce Canyon*)

AE - Ammunition ship (volcanos, deities of war, and things related to explosives; USS *Shasta*)

AF - Store ship (stars; USS *Arcturus*)

AFS - Combat store ship (stars or counties; USS *San Jose*)

AGMR - Major communications relay ship

AGS - Survey ship

AH - Hospital ship (words that suggest the ship's mission; USS *Repose*)

AK - Cargo ship

AO - Oilers (rivers with Indian names; USS *Hassayampa*)

AOE - Fast combat support ship (cities; USS *Sacramento*)

AOR - Replenishment oiler (cities; USS *Wichita*)

AR - Repair ship (mythical characters; USS *Hector*)

ARS - Salvage ship

AS - Submarine tender (people who have contributed to submarine development, or mythological characters; USS *Sperry*)

ASR - Submarine rescue ship (birds)

ATF - Fleet ocean tug (Indians and Indian words; USS *Seneca*)

CA - Heavy cruiser (cities; USS *Newport News*)

CG - Guided missile cruiser (cities; USS *Oklahoma City*)

CGN - Nuclear-powered guided missile cruiser (first ones were cities, now states; USS *California*)

CV - Attack aircraft carrier (famous ships of the past, famous battles, Presidents — now on an individual basis; USS *Coral Sea*)

CVN - Nuclear-powered attack aircraft carrier (no set naming pattern; USS *Enterprise*)

DD - Destroyer (Navy and Marine Corps heroes, members of Congress, and Naval leaders; USS *Carpenter*)

DDG - Guided missile destroyer (same as destroyer)

FF - Frigate (same as destroyer)

FFG - Guided missile frigate (same as destroyer)

LLC - Amphibious command ship (mountains and mountain ranges; USS *Mount Whitney*)

LKA - Amphibious cargo ship (cities or counties; USS *Tulare*)

LPD - Amphibious transport dock (cities; USS *Ogden*)

LPH - Amphibious assault ship (famous amphibious battles; USS *Iwo Jima*)

LSD - Landing ship dock (cities and counties; USS *Anchorage*)

LST - Tank landing ship (same as LSD)

MSO - Minesweeper, ocean ("logical, fine-sounding words;" USS *Gallant*)

SS - Submarine (sea creatures; USS *Wahoo*)

SSBN - Nuclear-powered fleet ballistic missile submarine (famous American leaders; USS *Mariano G. Vallejo*)

SSN - Nuclear-powered submarine (older ones after sea creatures, most recent after cities; USS *Haddock*)

YTB - Yard tug boat (Indians or Indian words; USS *Pokogan*)

USS *Seawolf* (SSN-575) ▾

US/1957/3,765 dt sur 4,200 dt sub/337 ft/ 28 ft/23 ft sur/20+ kts sur 20+ kts sub

Seawolf was the second nuclear submarine built for the U.S. Navy. She was built at the same time as the world famous *Nautilus*, to test a competitive nuclear reactor design. The *Seawolf* is slower than most modern nuclear submarines and, since 1969, has been used primarily for research. She is home-ported at Mare Island Naval Shipyard at Vallejo.

(Official U.S. Navy Photograph)

USS *San Francisco* (SSN 711)

US/1980?/6,000 dt sur 6,900 dt sub/360 ft/ 33 ft/32 ft sur/30+ kts sub

Two previous Navy ships, both distinguished cruisers, have borne the name *San Francisco*. The third ship to bear that name is under construction as this book is written. The new *San Francisco* is an attack nuclear submarine. Once called hunter-killers, attack submarines are designed primarily to seek out and destroy enemy submarines. With nuclear power, submarines like the *San Francisco* are capable of cruising silently beneath the surface for months at a time. Because they are deployed and remain submerged for long periods, each modern nuclear boat has two full crews. While the Blue crew is at sea, the Gold crew remains ashore for rest, recreation, and training.

(Official U.S. Navy Photograph)

USS *Enterprise* (CVN-65)
US/ 1961/ 90,000 dt/ 1,123 ft/
257 ft/ 37 ft/ 280,000 hp/ 30+ kts

The *Enterprise* is the world's largest warship, and was the first nuclear-powered aircraft carrier built. Eight nuclear reactors power her four five-bladed propellers. In 1964 the *Enterprise* circumnavigated the globe, a voyage of over thirty thousand miles, without taking on fuel or provisions. She is homeported at Naval Air Station, Alameda. She carries eight different kinds of aircraft and a crew of more than five thousand, which consumes over fifteen tons of food each day.

(Official U.S. Navy Photograph)

(Official U.S. Navy Photograph)

USS *Carpenter* (DD-825)

US/ 1949/ 3,540 dt/ 390 ft/
41 ft/ 21 ft/ 2 screws/ 33 kts

The *Carpenter* is one of the Navy's older destroyers. She is frequently used as a Naval reserve training ship, embarking West Coast citizen sailors for refresher courses in naval technology. The *Carpenter* is a fully operational combat ship with missiles and torpedos for anti-submarine warfare (ASW). She saw duty in naval gunfire support and coastal patrol during the Viet Nam War. In this photograph the *Carpenter* is seen on a reserve training cruise to Hawaii.

USS *Excel* (MSO-439) ▶

*US/ 1955/ 735 dt/ 172 ft/
36 ft/ 13.6 ft/ 2 screws/ 14 kts*

Ocean minesweepers like the *Excel* are specially constructed of nonmagnetic materials. The hull is wood and the diesel engines are built with nonmagnetic stainless steel to minimize the danger of the ship detonating magnetic mines. When "sweeping," heavy cables are streamed behind the ship. High voltage currents in the cables set up magnetic fields along their length which cause the mines to be detonated well astern of the ship. In addition to her combat duties, *Excel* has also hosted Bay Area clergymen for the annual Blessing of the Fleet on Opening Day of the yachting season.

(Official U.S. Navy Photograph)

(Official U.S. Navy Photograph)

USS *Kiska* (AE-35) ▲

*US/ 1972/ 18,088 dt/ 564 ft/
81 ft/ 28 ft/ 20 kts*

Kiska is a modern ammunition ship capable of transferring ammunition either by fast cable systems or helicopters. Where individual shells and powder bags were once passed hand-to-hand, mechanical systems now handle whole pallet loads or completely assembled missiles. Elevators fed by fork lifts connect the ship's hold to its deck, where power-operated deck transporters move ammunition to the transfer points. The *Kiska* can also carry two twin-engined helicopters. She is homeported at the Naval Weapons Center, Concord.

Tugs, Towboats, and Barges

Hull

Tugs are the football players of the maritime industry. To withstand the abuse, tug hulls are built with especially heavy materials. Thick double and triple wood planking was once the rule, but now most tugs are made of heavy steel plates. In addition many tugs, particularly those used in docking, are fitted with the split-pipe rub rails that are welded along the hull above the waterline for additional strength. One look at the dents on the rub rails shows just how much contact there is in the tug business.

In simplest terms, tugs either pull or push. When pushing, they "put their bow to it." As a result, tugs have nearly straight bow profiles so they can push against ships and barges without riding up. But even though the bows are fairly standard, there are subtle differences in design that can help you to guess the relative age of a tug. If you look at a lot of tugs, at San Francisco's Pier 9 for example, you will begin to notice that some have more pointed bows than others. The tugs with rounded bows will also seem stouter. Round-nosed, fat tugs are modern, and pointy-nosed skinny tugs are older. The reasons for the increased stoutness are greater fuel capacity and more stability, which together make the tugs more versatile.

The forward two-thirds of a tug hull below the waterline is full and tends toward a flat bottom. The after third cuts sharply up to the stern. This shape allows maximum water flow through the tug's screws and past the rudders. Most modern tugs are twin screwed with large, multibladed propellers. The rudders are arranged so that the tug can turn in a minimal distance, as well as give a sideways push when necessary. Some of the Bay's shallower draft tugboats have circular shrouds around their propellers, called Kort nozzles, which increase the effective thrust of their screws.

Fenders

At first glance, tugs look like they have just emerged from a bath in a junk yard. Fenders made of old tires seem to hang everywhere. Tug fenders have traditionally been fashioned from discarded materials, but the tire is a relatively recent innovation. Before the tire, old manila fiber hawsers were laboriously knotted into rope fenders. Both labor costs and the shift to synthetic fiber hawsers have made the rope fenders impractical.

Fenders serve two functions. The most obvious is to protect the tug from damage when it's maneuvering close alongside a tow. The second function is best understood by a simple experiment. Rub two pieces of metal together. They slip over each other fairly easily. Now put a piece of rubber between them. The rubber tends to hold the two pieces of metal in place beside each other. Tug fenders operate the same way. When the tug gives a mighty push against a steel hull the fenders keep it from slipping.

Side fenders are generally old heavy-duty truck or tractor tires. They ride on the rub rail and are held in place by chain, cable, or pieces of old hawser. Bow fenders have to deliver the full force of the tug, and are therefore much sturdier. Bow fenders are made by tightly lacing sections of old tires onto heavy cables. The assembly is then shaped for the individual tug and securely fastened to steel fittings on the bow.

Deckhouse

Except for tow boats, American tugs have traditionally had long, low deck-houses to provide living space and a galley for the boat's crew. Because of the tug's minimal freeboard, the deckhouse is vulnerable to seas coming over the rail. The hatches are the most likely spot to take water, so they are fitted with steel doors that are fastened shut with heavy latches called *dogs*. Generally the hatches are kept closed when the tug is operating, unless additional interior ventilation is needed.

Tugs with long deckhouses often have a second steering station on top of the after part of the deckhouse. From there the tug captain can watch the stern hawser at critical times without turning away from the boat's controls. Only minimum controls are included at the outside steering station: a wheel or hydraulic steering lever, engine speed and direction controls, and a searchlight.

Perched atop the deckhouse is the wheelhouse, the nerve center of the tug. Inside are several radios, radar, engine and rudder controls, whistle and horn levers, and a confusing array of switches and gauges. The wheelhouse is a good indicator of how a tug is used. Harbor tugs have narrow, low wheelhouses so they can fit in under the flair of a ship's bow. Tow boats have high wheelhouses with windows all the way around so the Captain can see his tow from any direction. Oceangoing tugs are not generally used for docking, so their wheelhouses can be wider, with more room for navigation equipment.

Deck Gear

Tugs are utility boats. While their primary job is to tow or push, they can be asked to do those two simple things in any number of ways. Versatility is therefore important in a working tug. Nowhere is that more apparent than in the deck gear, the equipment used to handle the lines that attach the tug to its tow. The bits, winches, capstans, and other gear must be able to handle the mightiest force the tug can deliver, while being easily and quickly used by the boat's crew. As a result a tug's deck gear is extremely sturdy and simple.

Fairleads change the direction of pull on a line without undue friction or wear. They are common on all types of vessels, but tugs have two that are uniquely theirs — the bull's nose and Nosman pins.

The **bull's nose**, common on harbor tugs, resembles the ring often seen in the nose of a prize bull. When a tug is docking a ship using its bow, the hawser is passed first through the bull's nose, then up to the ship. With the hawser through the bull's nose, it's much easier for the tug's crew to handle because they are pulling back rather than down.

Norman pins are most common on tugs that haul barges offshore. Essentially they are two parallel pins on the stern that keep the hawser or tow cable centered on the stern. Keeping the tow line centered makes steering easier.

Bitts are used to secure lines and hawsers aboard the tug. They are generally made of two vertical pieces of heavy duty steel pipe. They are fastened to the deck with a heavy mounting plate, and are capped at the top to keep the lines from slipping off. Tow lines and hawsers are never tied; instead, they are laced over the bitts in such a way that the line tension and friction hold them in place.

"H" bitts are a special adaptation of the normal bitts that have been successful in tugs. The standard uprights are connected by a single cross-member, which extends out from either side. This arrangement makes it possible to secure a line or a hawser from any direction.

Capstans are located in the bow and on the afterdeck in line with the bitts. These hourglass-shaped drums are used to take in tow lines or to put them under tension. They are driven by either hydraulic or heavy-duty electric motors. A deck hand must pay careful attention to how the line is feeding and to the motion of both the tug and the tow when working at the capstan. Sometimes he must snub the line quickly on the bitts to prevent losing the line he has just taken in.

Many tugs have large single or double drum **towing winches** aft of the deckhouse. These winches are used when the tug is towing a barge astern. The cables on the drums lead aft over the stern and on to a shock line, which is in turn connected to the towing bridle on the barge. Tow lines do not stretch straight between a tug and its tow. Instead they hang beneath the water in an arc called a **catenary.** In shallow water or close quarters the tow line is shortened so that it doesn't drag on the bottom and so that the tug has maximum control of the tow. In deeper water offshore, the tow line is payed out so the tug and its tow can ride better. Towing winches, particularly the newer automatic winches that maintain constant tension on the line, make the job of adjusting tow line length and catenary relatively easy.

51

Lines and Hawsers

Nowhere has modern technology been more important to tugs than in the lines they use to handle tows. For most of the more than one hundred years tugs have been around, manila fiber rope was all that was available. It was used for hawsers, heaving lines, and just about everything else. When it was too worn to be used safely, it was knotted into fenders and used until the last fibers were gone. But that was before the age of synthetic fibers like nylon.

Today there is a rope fiber for every use, and in many cases best for only that one use. Nylon, for instance, is three times as strong as the same size manila rope, resists wear better, and stretches. The fact that it stretches makes it particularly suitable for use as towing hawsers that have to absorb the shock of a rocking barge. The fact that it stretches also makes it unsuitable for docking work because the tug has to be held absolutely tight to the ship it's working. For both docking and alongside towing, dacron or polypropylene is preferred because they are almost as strong as nylon without the stretch. Polypropylene's special virtue is that it floats, which makes it very handy in some salvage situations or on jobs where the line might foul the propeller. But when too heavy a strain is taken on a synthetic line it vibrates like a cat's erratically twitching tail, then parts with a resounding crack.

The horsepower of newer offshore tugs and the size of the barges they can tow complicate the line situation even more. Manila, even in a very large hawser, can't stand the strain, nor can any of the other fiber lines. Wire rope is used, sometimes as thick as two inches or more. Wire rope is far too heavy to be handled by hand. The wire is coiled onto large-diameter towing winches.

Hawsers are thick fiber lines. Technically a hawser is any line that is over 4½ inches in circumference, but as a practical matter, it may not be easy for the boatwatcher to measure precisely. As a working definition, if it looks like you could put your thumb and index finger around it without their tips touching, call it a hawser. If you think they would touch, call it a line. Most of the lines used on tugs are hawsers.

Heaving lines are small, seldom over half an inch in diameter. Hawsers are too heavy and clumsy for throwing, but the lines have to be passed from the tug to its tow. One end of the heaving line is tied to the hawser and the other is thrown to the ship or tow. The hawser can then be hauled aboard with relative ease. Sometimes the throwing end of a heaving line has a baseball-sized knot with a weight in it called a monkey's fist. The monkey's fist makes it possible to throw the line farther and more accurately.

Oceangoing Tugs

(Photo courtesy Crowley Maritime Corp.)

Most tugs are capable of taking an occasional tow offshore. Tugs are utility boats and they go where the work is. But those that make their living in the less than peaceful waters of the Pacific are a breed unto themselves. By brute force alone they are the giants of the tug business, ranging from 2,000 to 9,000 horsepower. They can haul barges with payloads that rival those of medium-sized freighters. Tugs working out of San Francisco Bay haul containers, oil, urea for fertilizer, paper products, and many other bulk cargos from Alaska, British Columbia, Hawaii, and other points near and far.

When first seen, oceangoing tugs are hard to distinguish from harbor tugs. The first thing you notice is that they are bigger, between 90 and 140 feet long, and wider than harbor tugs. If a harbor tug happens by you will notice that the ocean tug has a shorter deckhouse, and that its wheelhouse is wider. Behind the shorter deckhouse is a long, uncluttered afterdeck that looks large enough for the crew to play shuffleboard.

Oceangoing tugs carry from five to fifteen people, with the most common crew size being eight. Most of the "outside" tugs built in the last ten years are completely automated, which makes safe operation possible while at the same time making the crew's jobs easier. But don't be misled. If you're looking for an easy, relaxed job on the water, most tug crews will recommend that you look elsewhere.

Sea Lion

US/ 1965/ 190 gt/ 121 ft/
32 ft/ 13 ft/ 2,800 hp/ 1 screw

Sea Lion is one of a large fleet of ocean-going tugs owned by the Crowley Maritime Corporation. She is small by present standards, but her 100,000 gallons of fuel and 18,000 gallons of water make her quite suitable for ocean towing. There are crew accommodations in both the forecastle and the deckhouse. Crowley Maritime Corporation has been an active part of the Bay scene since the days of pulling boats and water taxis.

53

(Photo courtesy Crowley Maritime Corp.)

Sea Swift

US/ 1968/ 194 gt/ 136 ft/
37 ft/ 17 ft/ 7,000 hp/ 2 screws

Sea Swift is one of many large ocean-going tugs that came into their own during the development of Alaska's North Slope oil fields. Her large driving engines are supplemented by two diesel engines to power her deck gear, and two large electrical generators. *Sea Swift* and her sisters haul tremendous ocean barges throughout the world. They make regular trips between Hawaii and San Francisco with container barges, and bring warehouse barges loaded with urea from Alaska.

Harbor Tugs

The most commonly seen tugs on the Bay are harbor tugs, the go-anywhere do-anything workhorses of the harbor. Harbor tugs have been part of the Bay since 1851. Indeed, many of the ships that called on the Bay in the early days would have found maneuvering very difficult without the tugs. Before the tugs, a ship had to strike its sails and wait at anchor. When winds and current permitted, the ship was pulled into the dock by a long boat rowed either by the ship's crew or by men who had been hired by the ship's agent. As ships grew larger, rowing them into their docks became impractical, but the helpful steam-powered harbor tug was there to do the pulling that oars couldn't.

Today's harbor tugs are equally handy. They dock ships of all sizes in all weather and tides. But docking, or ship assist, is only part of the harbor tug's responsibilities. They also push and "tug" the myriad barges associated with San Francisco's vast Bay. Bunkering barges must be hauled from the refineries to ships that need refueling. Molasses, oil, and other lighter cargos have to be hauled to the appropriate terminals. Dredge spoils, rock for breakwaters, old pilings, cranes and parts for bridges — you name it. If it moves on the Bay, the chances are good that harbor tugs haul it. It's a rare moment that a harbor tug can't be seen somewhere on the Bay doing its yeoman's job.

To the men who operate them, there are two kinds of tugs — large harbor tugs and small harbor tugs. That seems simple enough, but wait. The tugmen aren't talking about the size of the boat. When they say a tug is small, they mean it has a small engine or engines with a total horsepower of less than 1,200. Large harbor tugs are in the 2,000 horsepower range, with some even larger. Small-sized tugs generally have less horsepower and larger tugs more, but not always. Maddeningly for the boatwatcher, some small harbor tugs are every bit as long as their large harbor tug sisters. Sometimes you have to know the individual tug to be sure.

Panama ▲
*US/ 1911/ 21 gt/ 46.7 ft/
14 ft/ 6 ft/ 125 hp/ 1 screw*

Lobos ▲
*US/ 1953/ 25gt/ 45 ft/
12.5 ft/ 5 ft/ 10 kts*

Lobos is one of the classic small harbor tugs on the Bay. She is owned and operated by the Army Corps of Engineers. The Corps is responsible for maintaining the navigability of the Bay's waterways. Lobos is part of the fleet of vessels that deal with one of the Bay's bigger naviga-tion hazards, the logs that come down the inland rivers. Lobos is always on patrol or responding to notices of log sightings. At the end of her day she will have a sizable flotilla of logs streaming behind her as she makes her way back to her Sausalito base.

The Panama is the oldest operating tug on the Bay. She was built in San Francisco in 1911, and is now operated by the Slackwater Towboat Company out of Richmond's Santa Fe Channel. As long as there is no wind or current, the company proclaims that the Panama "will haul anything anywhere." Because of the limited horsepower of her marvelous old diesel engine, the Panama's tows are generally limited to recreational vessels and houseboats.

Western Panther ▲
*US/ 1948/ 54 gt/ 68.5 ft/
23 ft/ 7 ft/ 1,000 hp/ 11 kts*

Paul P. Hastings ▲
*US/ 1945/ 569 gt/ 142 ft/
33 ft/ 16 ft/ 1,600 hp*

The *Paul P. Hastings* is the last active railroad tug on the Bay. She serves the Atchison, Topeka and Santa Fe route between Richmond and San Francisco's China Basin. Built as an Army steam tug at the end of World War II, she was acquired by Santa Fe and put to work on the Bay in 1947. She was converted to her present diesel power in 1967. The tall pilothouse for seeing over freight cars and the seven-man crew are characteristic of railroad tugs. The *Hastings* and its barge can be watched from the street near Pier 54.

Steadily pushing with her single screw, the *Panther* helps dock a Chinese chemical tanker. Two hawsers have been led through the tug's bull's nose to the ship's bow, allowing the *Panther* to push or pull in any required direction. The *Panther* is equipped with flanking rudders forward of the screw to give maneuvering control when backing. Small harbor tugs like the *Panther* are often found tucked next to the bow of docking ships.

Sea Horse ▲

*US/ 1944/ 182 gt/ 95.6 ft/
24 ft/ 10.5 ft/ 1,200 hp*

Siegfried Tiger ▲

*(Tiger) US/ 1966/ 178 gt/ 88 ft/
31 ft/ 12 ft/ 2,000 hp*

Siegfried Eagle ▲

*(Eagle) US/ 1961/ 98 gt/ 67 ft/
21 ft/ 9.4 ft/ 1,200 hp*

The *Tiger* and the *Eagle* are versatile small and large harbor tugs respectively. They are used mainly to assist docking ships, but can easily haul barges both on the Bay and offshore. In this bow and stern view you can see the characteristic harbor tug narrow wheelhouse on the *Eagle*, and a heavy-duty towing winch tucked under the after part of the deck-house on the *Tiger*. The white box and canopy atop the port side of the *Tiger's* deckhouse is an after steering station, used occasionally when the tug is pulling rather than pushing. The *Tiger* and *Eagle* are operated by Western Tug & Barge, and can often be seen on the west side of Pier 9 in San Francisco.

In profile, the *Sea Horse* is fairly typical of the Red Stack harbor tug fleets owned by Crowley Maritime Corporation. There is an after steering station atop the back of the long deckhouse. The deck-house is protected by three round fenders when the tug is working in under the flare of a ship's bow. Red Stack tugs like the *Sea Horse* are seen all over the Bay, docking ships and hauling barges.

Tow Boats

Because of the huge double push knees on their bow, tow boats are the most easily recognized of all the tugs on the Bay. Locally known as "pusher boats," tow boats spend most of their lives pushing rather than pulling flat-sterned barges, which is the reason for the strange shape of the push knees. In order to get the skipper up where he can see over a barge, both the deckhouse and wheelhouse are high, making the tow boat seem tall for its length. An after steering station is unnecessary because the wheelhouse has windows on all sides.

Tow boats often work in shallow water, so they have a shallower draft than do harbor tugs. The shallower draft also means that a tow boat will be less powerful than a harbor tug of the same horsepower. To compensate for the loss of power many of the tow boats have special shrouds around their screws called Kort nozzles, which increase the

effective thrust of the screws by about twenty percent. The Kort nozzles, in combination with special rudders, also increase the maneuverability of the tow boats.

American River ◄
US/ 1961/ 134 gt/ 64 ft/ 26 ft/ 8 ft/ 800 hp

Tow boats like the *American River* spend most of their time securely fastened to the stern of their tows. In this position it is essential that the boat and its tow be firmly anchored to one another as a single unit, so that the tow can be maneuvered by the tow boat. The tires along the side and stern fender strake indicate that she can tow on the hip or astern when necessary to round tight bends in a river, or when seas get especially rough. The tow boat design and small horsepower limit the *American River* to work inside the Gate.

59

Barges

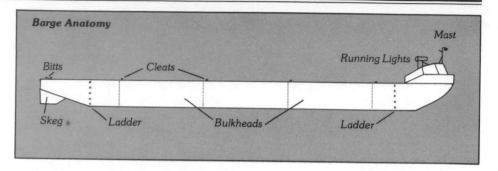

Barge Anatomy

Mast

Running Lights

Bitts

Cleats

Skeg

Ladder

Bulkheads

Ladder

Although they are often taken for granted even by those who work with them, barges are among the most efficient and useful watercraft afloat. Over the years they have been pushed and pulled by strong men, horses, sail, long poles, and anything else that would work. Today they are hauled by tugs.

Barges have chunky, ungraceful lines, and more often than not look like rusty hulks. They are also slow and hard to maneuver even in the best of circumstances. Seldom loved like other boats, they are nevertheless appreciated in the maritime industry for their own special quality — barges are inexpensive to build and maintain. Some barges may seem quite expensive, but when they are compared to ships doing the same job the cost of a barge seems almost insignificant.

Barges come in all sizes. Most are longer than 60 feet, with the upper limit for those normally seen on the Bay

being 400 feet, almost as long as many of the ships on the Bay. Barges carry almost anything. Huge tanker barges take Alaskan crude oil from tanker ships at Anchorage 9 to the refineries. Bunkering barges carry fuel from the refineries to ships all over the Bay. One barge loads molasses at Oakland's Matson terminal and takes it to the sugar plant at Crockett. There is even a barge that hauls railroad freight cars from Richmond to San Francisco.

Barge Anatomy

One of the beauties of the barge is that it is simple. Basically it's a floating platform with deck hardware for holding

cargo and tow lines, plus ground tackle for anchoring. Frequently both the bow and stern are raked, but if the barge is pushed very often the stern is left flat. Oceangoing barges tend to have spoon-shaped bows, which are better suited for pounding through ocean waves. Paddle-shaped structures may be attached to the stern rake to help control *yawing*, or swerving from side to side while under tow. On the side of the barge, near both the bow and the stern, ladders are inset into the hull. These ladders are most often seen on oceangoing barges, and are used by the tug crew to board the barge.

Towing Barges

While there are many modifications of each, there are three basic methods of towing barges — ahead, pushing, and "on the hip." When towing ahead, the tug pays out a tow line from its stern. The tow line is then attached to the barge by a bridle that is in turn attached to bitts on the outside edges of the barge's bow. The connection between tug and barge is not always apparent, however, because the tow line normally rides below the surface of the water.

When pushing, the tug is firmly anchored against the stern of the barge. For this reason most of the harbor, Bay, and river pushing is done by tow boats with specially-built push knees. The tow boat begins by positioning itself against the stern of the barge. Lines are then connected between the after corners of the barge and the stern quarters of the tow boat. Other lines may be used to reinforce the outside lines. When the

slack is taken up in the outside lines by mechanical ratchets or a towing winch, the tow boat becomes an integral part of its tow. This kind of tow is particularly suited for rivers and shallow water areas, where maneuvering is critical.

Towing on the hip is most commonly seen on the open waters of the Bay, where maneuvering room is less critical. If you watch long enough you will see tugs attached from stem to stern alongside barges, but the majority will be attached near the stern. As in pushing, the tug is firmly anchored to the barge. The pattern of lines to accomplish the anchoring depends on the deck gear of both the tug and barge, as well as the habits of the crew. The critical factor is for the tug to have control over the barge's stern.

Nanoose Carrier
Canada/ 1966/ 9,911 gt/ 360 ft/ 82 ft/ 14.3 ft

This barge looks like it should carry almost anything other than what it does, paper. Here is an example of the growth and development that has happened in the ocean barge trade. Paper is not as time-critical as television sets or cars, so speed is not the first consideration in its transportation. On the other hand, paper is fragile, which makes cargo safety more critical. The barge is arranged so that cargo handling equipment can drive right into the barge, minimizing the handling of the paper. The *Nanook Carrier* and her sister barge *Nanook Carrier* regularly call at San Francisco's Pier 15.

Scow Barge ▶

(Tug *Frank White* with hopper barge on the hip.)

Scow barges take their name from their pole boat ancestors, though it's hard to imagine even a large crew poling them anywhere. They are the utility barges of the Bay, carrying low-value bulk cargos such as rock for breakwaters, pilings, and dredge spoils. If it's dirty and heavy, the scow is the barge for the job. Their trade is so arduous that the scow barges are the least respectable-looking vessels on the Bay, but they do their job.

Hopper barges are a very special type of scow barge with doors on the bottom, used primarily in dredging. The barge is loaded by a dredge, then towed off to a dump site by a tug. At the dump site a tug crewman opens the doors and spills the barge's contents into the water, where the currents will carry them out to sea.

450-1▲

*US/ 1975/ 8,123 gt/ 400 ft/
99.6 ft/ 24 ft*

Tankers up to fifty feet deep, most carrying Alaska crude oil, are frequent callers on the Bay, but the upper Bay is too shallow for them to get to the refineries when they are fully loaded. They have to unload, or lighter off, some of their cargo before they can go up-river. Three huge barges, Crowley Maritime's *450-1, 450-2,* and *450-5,* have proven very handy for offloading the crude, up to 120,000 barrels per load. The barges were specially outfitted for the lightering operation at Merritt Shipyard in Oakland.

Alaska ▲

*US/ 1976/ 10,127 gt/ 395 ft/
80 ft/ 24.3 ft/*

Looking like floating warehouses, Crowley Maritime's *Alaska* and her sister barge the *Oregon* carry urea, produced as a byproduct of Alaskan oil operations, to fertilizer plants near Stockton and Sacramento. On the return trip they carry palletized and container general cargo. She has 560,000 cubic feet of interior space, and room outside for containers and large items like prefabricated housing units.

Bunkering Barge ▲

Bunker fuel is used in both steam boilers and residual fuel diesels on merchant ships. Since ships use large amounts of bunker fuel, and shoreside space is valuable, pierside storage isn't practical. Instead, barges come alongside the outboard side of the ship so it can refuel at the same time it handles cargo. Bunkering barges are easy to recognize because they have hose lines in the center, right where the cargo would go if they didn't carry fuel.

Workboats

Day or night they are there, in fair weather and foul. If there is a job to be done on the Bay there is a workboat to get it done. During the Monday through Friday work week most of the boats you see on the Bay are workboats. Pile drivers repair old piers and sink the footings for new ones. Dredges fight the continuing battle of shifting sand and mud. There are workboats to "sweep up" hazardous debris, and others to ferry ship's crews back and forth to their anchored homes.

The variety of tasks performed by workboats is almost unlimited. Though their presence is masked by the horde of pleasure boats that crowd the Bay on weekends, the workboats are out there then too, doing the often unglamorous jobs that are vital to keep the port functioning.

Of Pilots and Their Boats

Imagine that you are a ship's captain coming into a strange harbor. You have all the navigation charts and electronic equipment necessary to get you into your berth. There is only one thing you lack. Mariners call it "local knowledge," the kind of savvy that comes from years of experience in one geographical area under all kinds of conditions. Is local knowledge necessary? Ask someone who is responsible for a multimillion-dollar ship and cargo. They will probably tell you that local knowledge is not absolutely necessary all the time, but it's certainly reassuring to have.

The men who provide local knowledge for visiting ships are called *pilots*. They ride on the ships they guide. While the ship's captain remains in command, the pilot takes control of the ship, the "con," for the period of time he is aboard. The responsibility is not new to the pilots because most are former ship's captains, or masters, themselves. Usually the pilot goes aboard while the ship is under way by climbing a narrow ladder that hangs over the ship's side.

There are three kinds of pilots on the Bay; bar pilots, inland pilots, and docking pilots. The bar pilots take ships in and out of the Bay between the Pilot Station eleven miles offshore and the eastern side of Alcatraz Island. Like a moat in reverse, the entrance to San Francisco Bay is guarded by a horseshoe bar of sand that often lies less than 30 feet below the surface. The Army Corps of Engineers maintains a narrow, 50-foot-deep shipping channel through the middle of the sand barrier. It's the bar pilot's job to take ships, some drawing 50 feet, back and forth through the shipping channel, as well as navigating the tricky currents of the Gate. The twenty-eight bar pilots handle eight thousand ships a year.

California

US/ 1977/ 130 gt/ 85 ft/ 27 ft/ 6.5 ft/ 700 hp/ 2 screws/ 13 kts

The *California* and her sister ship, the *San Francisco*, are the station boats for the San Francisco Bar Pilots. They alternate four-day periods at the Pilot Station eleven miles off the Golden Gate. The rubber strake around her side and the tires are to absorb the shock of coming alongside a ship to put the pilot aboard. The station boats are used continuously under all conditions, yet provide some comforts to the pilots while they wait for the next in-coming ship. When not at the Pilot Station, they can be seen between Piers 7 and 9 in San Francisco. The *Drake*, also seen at the same pier, is a backup station boat and utility boat.

Once a ship is in the Bay, the bar pilot leaves her. If the ship is bound for any place other than San Francisco or Oakland, it will probably take an inland pilot aboard. Inland pilots handle all ship movements through the Bay and up the rivers to Sacramento and Stockton. Strong, sometimes erratic currents coupled with narrow, steep-sided channels make the job of the inland pilot challenging. The upriver channels are limited to ships of less than thirty feet draft.

Docking pilots, as the name implies, dock and undock ships. Sometimes this is done by inland pilots, but not always. Tugs also supply docking pilots. In this case the senior man aboard the tug is the pilot, and he goes aboard the ship. The senior man left on the tug is called the first mate. The docking pilot commands and coordinates the docking tugs, line handlers, and the ship's engines.

Mallard ▲

US/ 1966/ 58 gt/ 65 ft/
16 ft/ 7.8 ft/ 1,000 hp/ 2 screws

The *Mallard* and her two sister ships are water taxis. Their primary job is to carry crew and provisions back and forth to the ships anchored in the Bay. They also ferry customs, immigration, and other government officials on calls to visiting ships. The water taxis are dispatched from San Francisco's Pier 9. They are regularly seen along the eastern San Francisco waterfront as they make their runs to Anchorage 9. The water taxis have a crew of two, an operator and a deck hand.

Inland Pilot ▲

US/   /   / 46 ft/
18 ft/ 4 ft/ 500 hp/ 22 kts

Inland Pilot and *California Pilot* are operated by the California Launch Service as pilot boats for the inland pilots, and occasionally as general service water taxis. Because they operate discontinuously inside the Bay, they have a single "operator" for crew. The heavy metal bars on the fore- and afterdecks are for the pilots to hold on to as they step aboard the ship's boarding ladder. California Launch Service operates the two boats out of the west side of San Francisco's Pier 9.

Phoenix ◀

US/ 1954/ 91 gt/ 89 ft/
19 ft/ 6 ft/ 1,100 hp/ 15 kts

The *Phoenix* is the guardian of the San Francisco waterfront. Her versatile fire-fighting capabilities include up to 9,600 gallons per minute of water through fourteen hose connections and five high pressure monitors, oxygen-starving foam, and carbon dioxide. The monitor on the after pilot house can be telescoped 50 feet in the air if necessary. The *Phoenix* also carries skiffs with portable fire pumps to go in under piers and put out "hot spots" once the major fire is out. Should an earthquake cut off part of the City's fire main system, as it did in 1906, the *Phoenix* can be attached to one of seven strategically-located manifolds so that her pumps can supply the pressure to fight landside fires.

Spill Spoiler I & II ▶

US/ 1975/ 47 gt/ 57 ft/
24 ft/ 7 ft/ 160 hp

The threat of oil spills has created a whole new era of marine technology. One of the most effective vessels, created and financed by the oil companies themselves, is the *Spill Spoiler*. The business part of the *Spill Spoiler* is two continuous belts that look like conveyor belts. As the *Spoiler* drives through a spill, the oil is soaked up by the belt like a sponge. On board, the oil is wrung out of the belt into tanks and the belt continues back to the water to pick up more oil.

The *Spill Spoilers* are powered by twin water jets. To back up, a cup-shaped "bucket" is placed behind the water jet, which changes its direction 180 degrees. The vessel's operator sits in the tiny pedestal wheelhouse on the forward part of the vessel. Whenever oil is being transferred from a tanker to a lightering barge, the *Spill Spoiler* is there. As a result, one *Spill Spoiler* can usually be seen at Anchorage 9 in the South Bay. When not at Anchorage 9, it can be seen in San Francisco next to the *Balclutha*.

Coyote▲

*US/ 1941/ 215 gt/ 97 ft/
30.5 ft/ 5.5 ft/ 9 kts*

The *Coyote* and her sister ship the *Raccoon* are converted Navy landing craft. Their job is to pick up the debris that floats around the Bay. Fortunately the tides tend to concentrate the debris in long bands. The *Coyote* follows along these bands, sweeping the debris into heavy steel nets that hang below the water in its open bow. On an average day she collects thirty tons of logs, derelict boats, tires, life jackets, and other assorted junk. The logs it removes from the Bay are easily capable of destroying a ship's propeller or stoving in a boat's hull. The log being lifted by the *Coyote's* crane in this picture is over 60 feet long.

MV *Las Plumas*▼

*US/ 1957/ 2,255 gt/ 362 ft/
59 ft/ 15 ft/ 2,100 hp/ 10 kts*

At 362 feet, the *Las Plumas* is one of the largest work boats on the Bay. Up to six times a day she makes her run between Oakland's Outer Harbor and her slip on the north side of the Army Street Terminal. When fully loaded she carries twenty-eight freight cars. She has a crew of seven, and can cruise at ten knots. At one time the *Las Plumas* had three screws, one forward and two aft like a double-ended ferry, but now operates on two aft screws as a single-ender. *Las Plumas* is Spanish for "The Feathers," the symbol of the Western Pacific Railroad, her owner.

69

Cranes

Floating cranes are like their shoreside equivalents in most respects. Their long booms, blocks and tackle are powered by one or more diesel engines and they are used to raise, lower, or move things horizontally. Cranes, because they handle heavy weights at the end of the boom, are easy to tip over. Shoreside cranes have counterweights on the back of the crane house and legs that can be extended to spread the load to the ground. Floating cranes also have counterweights, but use anchors in place of the legs. The anchors are set well away from the four corners of the crane's barge, and then the slack is taken up by winches.

Crane barges seldom have engines to move them from place to place. If they have to move, they call a tug. Sometimes a tug is also kept handy to move the anchors when the crane needs to change position. In some cases the crane operates without the use of anchors.

DB 300 ▲

US/ 1975/ 2,738 gt/ 255 ft/ 76 ft/ 14 ft

The *DB 300* is the largest crane on the Bay. When not in use for salvage or heavy construction she is berthed at Crowley Maritime Corporation's Merritt Shipyard in Oakland. She can lift three hundred tons, and is full-revolving. On board are quarters for sixty crewmen. When the giant kelp cutter *Kelstar* sank off Southern California, it was the *DB 300* that raised her.

Smith-Rice No. 4 ▲

US/ 1944/ 691 gt/ 120 ft/ 60 ft/ 9.6 ft

Number 4 is a typical barge-borne, versatile marine crane. It is used for everything from unloading ships to salvage and marine construction. The crane is towed from job to job by harbor tugs, but has equipment for making its own minor position adjustments. *Number 4* frequently takes part in bulk and break-bulk cargo operations in both San Francisco and Oakland, and is home based in the Oakland-Alameda Estuary.

Research Vessels

The hustle and bustle of the commercial sector tends to hide their presence, but research vessels are very much a part of the Bay scene. Navy oceanographic and communications research ships are frequent Bay visitors. Ships survey the underwater profile of the Bay for navigational charting, and there are submarines used exclusively for underwater research. Among the smaller craft are boats studying fisheries and water quality. Others teach young people the wonders of marine science.

While some research vessels are built specifically for research, most are converted from former military or commercial craft. The R/V *Eagle* was originally a minesweeper called the *Tanager* built of special metals so that it would be safe from magnetic mines.

(Photo courtesy Ocean Films Ltd.)

R/V *Eagle* ▲
US/ 1945/ 1,050 dt/ 221 ft/ 33 ft/ 9.5 ft/ 13 kts

The Research Vessel (R/V) *Eagle* is a converted Navy minesweeper uniquely designed to combine basic deep sea scientific research with commercial film production. Ocean Films Ltd. and Ocean Trust Foundation, owners of the *Eagle*, have dedicated her to creating a greater public and scientific understanding of undersea ecology. On-board equipment includes a complete laboratory and a deep diving sphere. The *Eagle's* San Francisco base is Pier 42.

R/V *Inland Seas* ▲
US/ 1944/ 111 gt/ 82 ft/ 20 ft/ 10 ft/ 450 hp/

Originally an air/sea rescue boat, the *Inland Seas* is now a floating marine biology laboratory. Classes go aboard the boat for the day so that scientists of the crew can teach the young students how to do marine research by having them work on some of the Marine Ecological Institute's ongoing projects to study the Bay. The *Inland Seas* is based in Redwood City.

Coast Guard

Tuna

*US/ 1970/ 28 gt/ 38.5 ft/
16 ft/ 5.9 ft/ 460 hp/*

The aluminum-hulled *Tuna* is one of several boats on the Bay operated by the California Department of Fish and Game. Used both on the Bay and offshore, the Fish and Game boats are employed in law enforcement patrols for the complex regulations governing both commercial and sport fisheries in the state, as well as in scientific game research. *Tuna* operates year-round out of the Berkeley Marina.

With a distinctive diagonal red stripe on each bow, the Coast Guard's cutters are among the most easily recognized boats and ships on the Bay. By a tradition dating back to the early days of its history, Coast Guard vessels are called cutters regardless of their design or function. The Coast Guard fleet seen on the Bay ranges from 378-foot, high-endurance coastal patrol ships to harbor patrol craft and motor whale-boats. Those with white hulls are used for search and rescue, law enforcement, or any of the Coast Guard's several other responsibilities. Black-hulled cutters are primarily used to maintain the "road signs" of navigable waterways, the vast system of buoys, lights, and other indispensable aids used by navigators to tell where they are. Red is reserved for the hulls of icebreakers.

The length of smaller Coast Guard boats is indicated by the first two digits of their hull numbers.

(Official U.S. Coast Guard Photo)

USCGC *Rush* (WHEC 723)
US/ 1969/ 2,716 dt/ 378 ft/ 43 ft/ 20 ft/ 29 kts

Cutters in this class combine an extended cruising range of ten thousand miles with a top speed of over 29 knots. The secret of their capability is a unique dual power plant — diesel engines for 17-knot cruising, and gas turbines for high speed. They are also able to stop in less than two ship lengths and have retractable bow thrusters for close quarters maneuvering. With a crew of 15 officers and 140 enlisted personnel, these cutters are primarily used to patrol the 200-mile Fishery Conservation Limit, and to search and rescue. The *Rush* and her sister ships normally tie up at Alameda just west of Mariner Square, and can be easily seen from Oakland's Jack London Square.

USCGC *Cape Carter*▲

*US/ 1953/ 105 dt/ 95 ft/
20 ft/ 6 ft/ 20 kts*

USCGC *Point Barrow* ▶

*US/ 1962/ 57 gt/ 82 ft/
17 ft/ 6 ft/ 2 screws/ 20 kts*

(Official U.S. Coast Guard photos)

The Coast Guard's 95-foot coastal patrol and offshore search and rescue cutters are all named after significant geographical capes *(Cape _____)*. Their 2,300 horsepower diesel engines are capable of driving the boats at 20 knots. These cutters are stationed at key locations along California's rocky coast. A stretcher, fire fighting equipment, and small outboard motor powered boat for search and rescue work can be seen along the *Cape Carter's* side and on her afterdeck.

Named after prominent points of land *(Point _____)*, the 82-foot cutters are offshore coastal utility boats. With their 1,700 horsepower diesel engines, they are capable of taking a stricken vessel in tow or speeding to a search and rescue mission. The hull is steel and the superstructure is aluminum. The pilothouse controls can be easily handled by a single operator. Eighty-two-foot cutters have a relatively small crew of eight.

(Official U.S. Coast Guard photos)

►Forty-One-Foot Utility Boat◄

US/   /1.4 dt/41 ft/
13.5 ft/4 ft/2 screws/24 kts

This boat is used primarily for law enforcement and search and rescue on the Bay. Twin 275-horsepower diesel engines power twin screws, and its semi-displacement hull allows it to cruise at 20 knots, with a maximum speed of 24 knots. The design of the aluminum hull has emphasized speed at the cost of the sea kindliness necessary for work offshore, limiting the boat to work inside the Gate. The utility boat generally has a crew of three.

◄Forty-Four-Foot Motor Lifeboat

US/   / 17.5 gt/ 44 ft/
12.7 ft/ 3.1 ft/ 2 screws/ 16 kts

This is one of the toughest little boats afloat. Designed for working in heavy seas and surf, it can be tumbled 360 degrees and keep going. It has a round-bottomed steel hull with a deeply flaired bow that tends to lift the boat over as well as to part oncoming waves. Motor lifeboats are used to guard the Golden Gate, which can be a nightmare of crashing surf, strong currents, and murky fog during the winter storm season. The boat normally has a crew of four.

75

USCGC *Comanche* (202) ▲
*US/ 1944/ 534 dt/ 143 ft/
33 ft/ 12.5 ft/ 13.5 kts/*

Comanche, originally built for the Navy, is a seagoing tug that pays periodic visits to the Bay from her base at Eureka in Northern California. She is powered by twin diesel engines of 750 horse-power each. Her tumblehome, stern bulwark, and amidships tripod clearly distinguish her as a seagoing tug. Tugs like the *Comanche* are particularly well suited to search and rescue work involving disabled ships. She has a crew of five officers and forty-two enlisted personnel.

(Official U.S. Coast Guard photos)

USCGC *Blackhaw* (390) ▼
*US/ 1944/ 935 dt/ 180 ft/
37 ft/ 13 ft/ 13 kts/ single screw*

Probably nothing is more important to safe navigation than the buoys, lights, signals, and other devices maintained by the Coast Guard to mark channels and hazards to navigation. Just one light out of commission or one buoy moved by stormy seas can spell disaster. The tender *Blackhaw* is designed to do maintenance and repair on ocean buoys. Smaller buoys like those seen on the Bay can be lifted aboard for necessary work. Large buoys like those used to replace lightships are towed in by the *Blackhaw* if they cannot be serviced on site. The Coast Guard also has a smaller 55-foot navigational aids boat on the Bay. Both vessels are stationed on the east side of Yerba Buena Island.

Passenger Vessels

Ferries

Although today's ferries are modern in all respects, they are somehow a link with the past — to the days before the bridges, when the communities that ring the Bay were connected by a grand fleet.

Here and there you can see remnants of the old ferry system. San Francisco's Hyde Street Pier, now home for the historical ships, was originally the terminal for the Sausalito and Berkeley ferries. The Ferry Building, which survived the 1906 earthquake, was and still is the center of ferry traffic. The now decaying Berkeley Pier carried traffic two miles out over the East Bay mud flats to where the ferries could dock. And the entrance to the Castro Point Marina was the toll booth for one of the last ferry lines superseded by the Richmond-San Rafael bridge in 1956.

Some of the grand ladies themselves are still with us as well, but unfortunately much of their grandeur is gone. The best preserved is the *Eureka* (see the chapter on Historical Ships), which floats proudly in her berth at the Hyde Street Pier. The *Klamath*, at San Francisco's Pier 5, is used for design studios and offices by Walter Landor Associates. Others have become private residences or restaurants, but most have been sold or simply set aside and left to decay.

All of the active ferries operate out of three communities in Marin County, and carry only passengers. Golden Gate Transit, a subdivision of the Golden Gate Bridge District, runs three boats from Larkspur in central Marin and one from Sausalito to the new terminal at the Ferry Building. Harbor Tours uses two cruise boats for morning and evening commute runs between the City and Tiburon. The remaining regular ferry connects Tiburon with Angel Island State Park, across Raccoon Strait.

GT *Sonoma, Marin, San Francisco*

US/ 1976/ 99 gt/ 152 ft/ 32 ft/ 5.8 ft/ 7,500 hp

These unusual ferries are among the fastest boats on the Bay. In spite of their size, their semiplaning hulls can glide through the water at better than thirty knots, even with a full load of passengers. From their airplane seats to their three gas turbine engines they are products of the Space Age. The conventional screw propellers have been replaced by water jets similar to those used in high speed ski-boats. For a fast trip on the Bay the "GTs" are unbeatable. They make regularly scheduled runs between the Ferry Building and Larkspur.

Golden Gate ▶
*US/ 1969/ 97 gt/ 103 ft/
29.5 ft/ 7 ft/ 1,100 hp*

The *Golden Gate* is a conventional diesel-powered, twin-screwed boat used to carry commuters and other ferry riders between Sausalito and San Francisco. The Bay had been without ferries for fourteen years when the transbay ferry was reinstated in 1971. The *Golden Gate* has a snack bar, and seating conducive to conversation with fellow passengers.

Angel Island ◀
*US/ 1975/ 98 gt/ 60 ft/
30 ft/ 5.7 ft/ 350 hp*

The little *Angel Island* has the shortest run of any active ferry on the Bay. The brevity of the run, however, is not reflected in the spirits of her passengers. *Angel Island* carries hikers, bicyclers, fishermen, swimmers, picnickers, and other outdoor enthusiasts back and forth between Tiburon and Angel Island State Park. She is also the only operating double-ended ferry on the Bay.

Harbor Tours, San Francisco

The Red and White Fleet at San Francisco's Fisherman's Wharf has introduced millions of people from all over the globe to the watery world of San Francisco Bay. As long as the weather permits, and that's most of the time, a Harbor Tour boat leaves Pier 43½ every half hour to forty-five minutes during the day. The boats run west along the Marina to Fort Point and the Golden Gate Bridge. After circling under the Bridge, they head east for close-ups of Alcatraz, Treasure Island, and a porpoise-eye view of the Bay Bridge. The return trip takes them north and west along the piers of San Francisco's waterfront. In addition to the "land sights," the cruise offers passengers a fantastic opportunity to see the working boats of the Bay in their own element.

There are eight boats in the Red and White Fleet. Seven are used for Bay cruises, ferry service, and charters. The *Harbor Tourist*, smallest member of the fleet, is used to ferry visitors back and forth between the City and Alcatraz Prison, now part of the Golden Gate National Recreation Area. All Harbor Tours boats are powered by diesel engines, and have twin screws. They are radar-equipped and in constant contact with the Coast Guard's Vessel Traffic Control Center to avoid unscheduled encounters with other boats.

Red and White Fleet

	Length— Feet	Passengers	Horsepower
Royal Star	129	650	900
Harbor Emperor	98	500	900
Harbor Prince	98	500	900
Harbor Queen	80	444	900
Harbor Princess	80	444	700
Harbor King	64	400	600
Harbor Tourist	64	210	400

Harbor Tourist

Harbor King

Harbor Prince

Charter Cruises

Chartering is popular for convention groups, businesses, and clubs. Under charter, a boat and its crew are retained for the exclusive use of the chartering group. Dinner cruises are the most popular. All of the charter companies boast excellent food that is either catered or prepared on board. Entertainment is also available for most charters. Combined with the romance of the Bay by night, charter amenities make for a memorable experience.

Hornblower Party Yachts has three boats available out of Berkeley's Marriott Inn or Pier 39 in San Francisco. Mariner Yacht Charters on Oakland's Jack London Square offers gourmet food on trips aboard the 68-foot motor yacht *Mariner II*. The *Angel Island* ferry can take up to 150 passengers out for a pleasure cruise when it is not obligated to ferry service.

Royal Star

And Harbor Tours' Red and White Fleet can be chartered in the evening for cruises of four hours or more. In addition, the *Royal Star* is used for dinner cruises on Thursdays, and for Sunday brunches that are open to both individuals and groups.

Many smaller pleasure boats are also available for charter throughout the Bay.

Some of these boats are formally associated companies or yacht brokers, but most are individuals. These boats may be chartered with crew or "bare boat." In most cases the smaller boats are limited to charter parties of six or fewer.

Fishing Boats

Hyde Street Pier is filled with historical vessels of many sizes. Among the smaller craft is a white and green double ender that sits, bright as a new penny, beside a fence near the ferry slip. It looks somehow out of place, from another part of the world, among all the old San Franciscans. Feluccas they were called, and they were the first commercial fishing boats on the Bay. Don't be misled by their size and apparent frailty; the feluccas were offshore boats that beat their way out through the Gate in rough weather and calm. While other kinds of boats were also used for fishing, they were hard to find among all of the lateen-rigged feluccas at Fisherman's Wharf. Hand lines, cod trawls, and crab trapping were the main fisheries. Shrimp, sardines, and oyster, now gone, came later.

Today the Bay has many commercial fishing fleets with a broad range of vessels in each. Their boats are made of wood, steel, aluminum, fiberglass, even concrete, and regardless of what they may look like, each is the best that available money could buy and "just a little too small." Diesel is the power of choice because the fuel is less expensive, and diesel engines are more reliable than gasoline engines. Most of the fishing boats seen on the Bay have tall, paired trolling poles on either side of the pilot house, because the majority of Bay fishermen chase salmon and albacore. Those not dedicated to trolling include bottom trawling draggers, long liners, crab boats, and a number of boats that concentrate on special fisheries.

Vibrant, active, and modern, the Bay's fishing fleets are still rich with tradition. Fishing here is mainly a family business, as it always has been. Most of the boats are individually-owned, and fished by their owners. The design of one of the most popular trollers, the Monterey Clipper, while unalterably a power boat, has incorporated much from its felucca ancestors. But the most important tradition is the fishing community itself. Each boat is a fiercely competitive, self-reliant unit, but taken together the fishing fleets are working cooperative communities.

Salmon Trolling

From mid-April through the end of September, salmon is king to the Bay's commercial fishermen. Boats of all sizes and descriptions tow their multihooked trolling gear through the warming Pacific waters, sometimes more than a hundred miles from shore. The salmon fishery is the home of the individual fisherman, man and woman alike. As often as not, single fishermen set out in individually-owned boats to pit themselves against the elements, depending completely on their own skill.

Salmon trollers range in size from small, open motor boats used for day fishing to big, expensive fishing machines capable of taking 40,000 pounds of salmon per trip. Most fall somewhere between the extremes, but all have telltale paired trolling poles and hydraulic, electric, or hand reels called "gurdies." Most boats fish six lines simultaneously, with three lines on each pole. Salmon trolling is done at one to

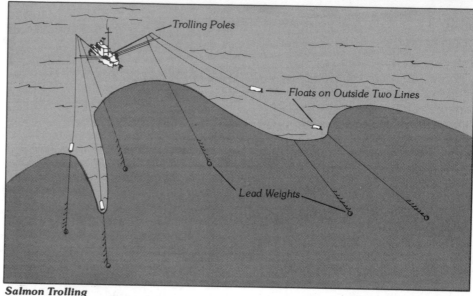

Salmon Trolling

two knots, which makes the boat quite vulnerable to rolling. To minimize roll and the attendant strain on both the fisherman and his gear, stabilizers called "flopper stoppers" are hung into the water from a point about one-third of the pole length from the boat.

Each troll line is heavily weighted with round lead sinkers, appropriately called "cannon balls," so that the lines stream below the surface. The heaviest weights, up to 65 pounds, are on the inside line, which hangs almost straight down. Beyond the first line, weight, length of line, and whether or not floats are

used vary with individual fishermen and conditions. Above the weights, each line bears five to eight leaders with shiny spinners and, sometimes baited, hooks. The number and spacing of the hooks depends on the species of salmon sought and the depth of the line.

The trolling gear used today has been developed through years of experimentation, and is fairly complicated when compared with the sport fisherman's rod and reel. Using the gear takes both experience and skill. Salmon trollers, like other fishermen, are rarely satisfied that they have complete mastery of their rig, or that the rig is all that it could be. Each season there are new lures, spinners, or baiting techniques to be tried, and new fishing grounds to be explored. Perhaps it's this open-ended room for experimentation and individual achievement that draws so many people to the salmon fishery. It certainly isn't the money; there are no rich salmon fishermen.

Eilene D
US/ | | / 35 ft/
12 ft/ 4 ft/ 7 kts

Eilene D is typical of the versatile, individually-operated salmon trollers on the Bay. When not in use, the trolling poles are fastened next to the mast. The boom hanging over the afterdeck is used for heavy-duty hauling. She has a six-ton capacity fish hold. The numbers found on the side of her pilothouse indicate that she fishes herring as well as salmon.

Albacore Trolling

The albacore is one of the smaller tunas and, because it is fished by trolling, it is one of the major alternative fisheries for the Bay's salmon fishermen. If the salmon aren't biting, or the season has ended, shifting over to fishing albacore can be done fairly easily. Unlike the salmon, however, albacore are seldom found closer than 50 miles from shore. Albacore are also lovers of warm waters. Unless ocean temperatures reach 57 degrees, there won't be any albacore. Exactly why is a secret known only to the fish. Because the presence of the less-valuable albacore generally corresponds with the salmon season, they are fished more actively when salmon catches are bad than in good salmon years.

Albacore are fished by surface trolling, with the boats traveling at six to eight knots. Four lines are fixed to each pole, and up to three are streamed from the stern. Each lightly-weighted line has one double, barbless hook lure that bounces

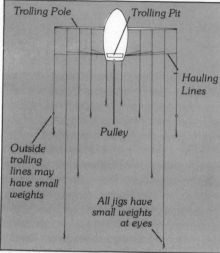

Albacore Rig

Esther Louise ▲

US/ 1973/ 12 gt/ 34.7 ft/
11.8 ft/ 4.5 ft/ 100 hp

at the surface of the water. Albacore are very cooperative. When they strike a lure they don't let go until the fisherman removes them from the hook on the boat. Because the gear is light and the fish average 20 pounds, the power gurdies associated with salmon trolling are unnecessary. Instead, a single power sheave is fixed behind the trolling pit and the line is coiled into baskets or boxes.

The *Esther Louise* is a salmon troller temporarily rigged for albacore. As the lines are hauled in by the single hydraulic sheave on the stern, they are fed into small boxes. When the fish reaches the boat it is hauled aboard by hand and deftly swung against a pin in the center of the trough leading forward from the stern. This separates the fish from the barbless hook, and the fish slides down to the deck. One of the nice features of albacore is that it can be iced directly without cleaning.

Long Lining

Long lining is probably the oldest method used by Bay fishermen. Once an important method of commercial fishing, today it is primarily an alternative to the salmon fishery. When the salmon are running, any time during the commercial season between mid-April and the end of September, it's a pure waste of time to look for long liners among the Bay's fishing fleets. There are long liners out there all year because the fish taken on long lines are delivered to market in better condition than those taken by other methods, but during the salmon season they are comparatively rare. In the Bay Area long lines are used primarily for several species of rock fish and sable fish, which is often marketed as butterfish.

Recognizing a working long liner is a matter of looking at the gear on deck. If there are round, almost flat baskets or metal buckets with long, coiled, multihooked lines in them you are looking at

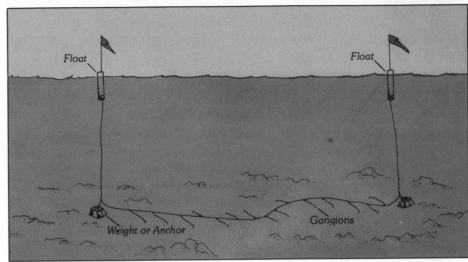

a long liner. Look closely at the hooks. There are 200 to 250 of them per line, each connected first to a leader called a *gangion* (pronounced "ganyon") and then to the main ground line. The gangions are evenly spaced along the line at 1½ to 3 foot intervals. When the line is carefully coiled, each hook in succession is sunk lightly into the sacking on the edge of the basket to await baiting.

The real test of skill in long lining, however, comes when the gear is "set" on the fishing grounds. First the length of the buoy line is determined from the water depth, then the line is thrown out with a marking pole, flag, light, radar reflector, or any combination thereof. Before the anchor (commonly a construction brick) goes over, the leading end of the first basket of baited line, or

Draggers

skate, is attached to the base of the buoy line. Then things start happening rapidly. As the anchor goes over, the boat pulls slowly away and the baited line pays out over the stern or is dropped over in a heap. One skate is attached to another until up to ten have been set in the string. Any tangles that occur as the gear is being set are left until the line is hauled for the catch. At the other end of the string another anchor is set at the bottom of a second buoy line with a floating marker.

Just from looking at the decks of a working long liner piled high with lines, you can see that the procedure must be repeated many times before all the gear is set. As a practical matter, long lining is not commonly undertaken by solitary fishermen. Even with a good crew it's a lot of hard work. But if the fish are there and everything else is right, it can have its rewards.

Locally known as "drag boats," "dragger boats," or simply "draggers," these bottom trawlers are the giants of the Bay fishing fleets. At the pier, draggers are most easily recognized by the rectangular metal "otter boards" or "doors" fastened to the gallows on either side of the stern. The drag net itself is wound on a large drum on the afterdeck.

Draggers fish the productive banks and other relatively shallow areas along the coast. The boat cruises over its fishing ground watching the electronic fish finder for any sign of fish schools. When a school is sighted, the boat is maneuvered into position and the net is "shot," or

Dragger Net

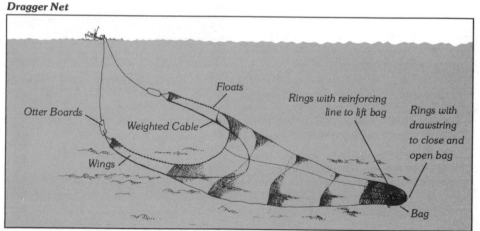

Otter Boards

Weighted Cable

Floats

Wings

Rings with reinforcing line to lift bag

Rings with drawstring to close and open bag

Bag

paid out, slowly over the stern. The otter boards are fastened to the wings of the net to keep it open while it's being trawled. Once enough line has been paid out that the skipper is sure the otter boards will remain on the bottom, the net is taken under tow.

Drag nets are generally towed for a half hour or more, but the fishermen like to keep the time as short as possible to minimize fouling and damage to the net. The net is hauled in several steps. First the otter boards are lifted off the bottom and brought up to the boat. When they have been secured, the net is shifted to the drum and hauled in, with the ground line leading the float line. Finally, the bag is boomed up over the side and positioned above the hold. With a tug on a special slip knot, the catch tumbles out of the bottom of the bag into the hold.

Draggers catch lingcod, sole, and sable fish, but the majority of their catch is rock fish or "rock cod."

Jack Jr.

US/ 1928/ 60 gt/ 72 ft/ 18.8 ft/ 7.9 ft/ 270 hp

Notice the winches at deck level on either side of the pilot house. These winches are used to haul in the otter boards on draggers. The winches as well as the net drum are powered by heavy-duty hydraulic motors. The *Jack Jr.*, like most net boats, is single screwed. She is homeported at Fisherman's Wharf.

Lampara Net Boat

A Mediterranean net design first introduced in California in 1905, the Lampara net is used primarily for anchovy and other bait fish. When a school of bait fish is spotted by watching feeding birds or by the electronic fish finder, the net is paid out around the school. The top of the net is larger than the bottom, and is attached to floats that keep it at the surface. The bottom of the net is attached to a weighted line. When the net is taken in tow, or hauled, the drag through the water causes the bottom to close.

The primary value of the Lampara net is that the fish can be contained in it without being killed. The net is hauled in beside the boat, where the fish are *brailed* (transferred with large dip nets) from the net into the water-filled hold. Water is continuously circulated through the hold tank so that the heavily concentrated fish are not killed by their own waste products.

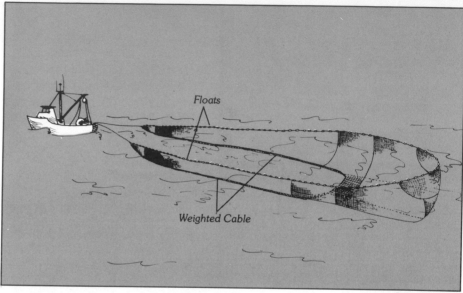

Floats

Weighted Cable

Lampara Net

Bait fishing is big business on the Bay because of the large commercial and sport markets for good bait. Bait boats are seen regularly along the San Francisco waterfront. Except for the very brief herring season, Lampara bait netting is the only commercial fishing operation readily observable on the Bay.

Buccaneer

Flagship of the Meatball Bait Company, *Buccaneer* is most familiar to thousands of Bay Area sport fishermen as the live bait boat. Concentrating primarily on the Bay, *Buccaneer* uses its Lampara nets to catch anchovies and keep them in good condition in three on-board circulating tanks. She is single screwed and operates out of the commercial fishing pier in Sausalito.

Crab Boats

For the millions of people who walk the steamy sidewalks of Fisherman's Wharf each year, to say crab is to say San Francisco. These tasty crustaceans have been a symbol of the waterfront for as long as most people remember. Once caught in nets, traps, and anything else that would work, today they may legally be taken only in traps. All of the crabs you see for sale on the street or in the market are males. That too is required by law. The females, which are smaller and lacking in meaty appeal, must be left to produce more males for market.

The traps, or "crab pots," are the key to the crab fishery. Developed through generations of experimentation, these devices have managed to put some of the work on the crabs themselves. The pots are round, about four feet across and less than half that high. The frame is welded steel rod, with several pieces of heavy cast iron across the bottom for weight and a half door on the

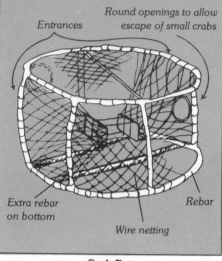

Crab Pot

top for removing the crabs. Netted with stainless steel wire, two funnel shapes extend into rectangular rod openings near the center. Each of the funnels is held in place by wires fastened to its opposite member, and between them hangs the perforated bait box. The

openings in the funnels are large enough to admit the meatiest crab, if he's determined, but they have a secret. As the crab enters, one or more wire rods hanging down from the funnel frame move effortlessly out of the way, then fall back into place over the opening once the crab is inside. The opening that was passed through with ease on the way in becomes impossible as a way out.

Undersize and female crabs can't be kept out, but they don't have to stay once they are inside. Since crabs attempt escape by going up, two holes just large enough for youngsters and females to slip through near the top allow the crabs to sort themselves into legals inside and sublegals outside. Nary a single fisherman finger need be lifted except to cull recent arrivals.

Thanks to these clever traps you can enjoy crab cioppino, crab Louis, crab cocktail, and countless other easy-to-appreciate delectables.

Johnny T.
*US/ 1969/ 28 gt/ 42.6 ft/
13.2 ft/ 6.5 ft/ 165 hp*

Among the telltale signs of a crab boat are the crab block for hauling in crab pots (the large pulley just aft of the deck-house), and the vertical wood rails fastened to the outside of the hull below the crab block, where the pots would chafe the boat. Of course, the pots themselves are the best indicator. Crab pots must be checked and re-baited regularly. The hazards of all this handling, as well as of sea conditions, mean that there are always pots on deck enroute to or from repair.

Historical Ships

San Francisco Bay is blessed with an unusually large collection of historical ships and boats. Old ferries are tucked here and there throughout the Bay. An entire fleet of old merchant ships is moored off the Benicia shoreline in windy Suisun Bay, and classic old windjammers can be seen on the Bay every day of the week. Best of all, the collection of historical ships open to the public is the largest on the Pacific Coast. Due to the dedicated efforts of a handful of Bay Area citizens, these ships were rescued from junk heaps, mud flats, and beaches, brought to San Francisco, restored, and opened to millions of appreciative people. Together with the Maritime Museum, the historical ships provide an invaluable link to the Bay's vibrant maritime history.

National Maritime Museum

There is probably no marine resource in the Bay Area more rewarding to visit than the San Francisco's National Maritime Museum. It is a living, vital link to the Bay it overlooks. Ship models from all ages give boatwatchers an opportunity to examine ships and their equipment in minute detail. Models, however, are only part of the displays. Key parts of many ships are combined with photographs to give visitors a sense of the size and "feel" of the ships. The stern and rudder of a scow schooner show the crude steering characteristics of those boats. An anchor windlass gives depth to one of the old Alaska Packer ships. A huge anchor, figureheads, harpoon, ship's wheel, a section of hull plating — pieces that transport visitors to the past. And everywhere there are photographs of the famous and not so famous ships that have called at the great San Francisco Bay.

The Museum is quartered in a building that resembles the bridge of a modern merchant ship. Even the sign bearing the name of the Museum is a replica of an old ship. Jutting out from the building is the transom of an old sailing ship by the name of *Maritime Museum*, with a homeport of San Francisco. She is a vessel worth visiting.

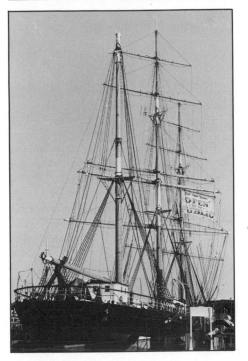

Balclutha

US/ 1886/ 1,689 gt/ 256.5 ft/
38.6 ft/ 22.7 ft

When the *Balclutha* was built in Scotland, steam was just proving itself and wind-powered ships still dominated the world's merchant fleets. There were no canals linking the great oceans. The only way to get from one to the other was to sail by way of the stormy Southern Oceans. To the ships bound for San Francisco, that meant rounding the tip of South America, treacherous Cape Horn. Those who made the trip, ships and sailors alike, were called Cape Horners, and commanded respect wherever they went.

The *Balclutha* made seventeen trips around the Horn carrying coal, guano, hardware, wine, wool, and other cargos. Her ports of call included Plymouth, Rotterdam, Le Havre, Rangoon, New Zealand, and San Francisco. But her world trader days came to a sudden end when she was sold into the Pacific lumber trade in 1899. Several years later she became part of the Alaska

Packers fleet in the canned salmon trade, and was eventually renamed the *Star of Alaska*. From 1933 until 1952, when she was laid up on the Sausalito mud flats, the *Pacific Queen* (ex *Star of Alaska*, ex *Balclutha*) was a sleazy exhibition ship owned by a former carnival stuntman. In 1954 she was bought by the Maritime Museum, renamed *Balclutha* and, through the volunteer efforts of both labor unions and businesses, restored to her present condition.

Each period in the *Balclutha's* long, busy life has been filled with adventure. These stories, as well as those of her sisters, are vividly told through displays, photographs, newspaper articles, and the ship's own spaces. Today the *Balclutha* is more than one of a handful of remaining Cape Horners. Like the Museum that saved her, she is a living link with the Bay's marine history.

Alma

US/ 1891/ 41 gt/ 59 ft/
22 ft/ 4 ft/ cross planked wood

Each year on a Sunday in May the Bay's classic old sailboats assemble off the St. Francis Yacht Club for the Master Mariner's Regatta. The race dates back to 1867 when the Bay's workboat skippers decided that a little racing competition would be fun. The race was not limited to workboats, but yachts generally fared badly against the day-in day-out seamanship of the workboat crews. Today most of the sailing workboats are gone from the Bay and the race, but not all.

Leading the Master Mariner's Regatta each year is a square-bowed, flat-bottomed hay scow that is to the Bay's waters what the cable car is to San Francisco's hills. The *Alma* is the last of a fleet of over three hundred boats that were uniquely able to use the heavy winds of the Bay yet navigate the shallow mud flats of the river channels entering the Bay. Loaded with up to 90 tons of hay, bricks, lumber, coal, or any other cargo

(Photo courtesy National Maritime Museum)

she could find, the *Alma* would raise her gaff-headed sails, lower her centerboard keel, and fly through the choppy Bay.

Once into the shallows the sails were often dropped and the centerboard raised. Like scows in other parts of the

Eureka
*US/ 1890/ 2,420 gt/ 300 ft/
78 ft/ 14 ft/*

country, the crew then took long lines and hauled the boat upstream by slogging through the muddy marshes.

Work on the hay-scow schooners was not glamorous. The crew not only had to get the boat back and forth, their trade was so small that they had to load and unload the cargo as well. But the life of the "tule-sailor" had its compensations. The captain generally owned the boat and traditionally shared the profits with his one- or two-man crew. When cargos were plentiful the pay was good, and cruises didn't mean long separations from family and friends.

The last scow schooner was built in the year of the great earthquake, 1906, but they continued as a vital part of the Bay scene until the 1920s. Decline came rapidly after that as new highways and the growth of trucking made the scows increasingly obsolete. Many of the

outmoded scows were stripped of their masts and converted to barges, but one by one they were simply used up.

In 1958 only the *Alma* survived. A mastless oyster shell dredge in the South Bay, the *Alma* continued to work eighteen hour days, six days a week. She had worked continuously for sixty-seven years, but new dredging equipment brought an end to her working life. The State of California was then assembling a fleet of historic ships for a maritime history park at the Hyde Street Pier. They acquired the *Alma* and pulled her off the Alviso mud flats in 1959.

Today, after being restored to her original scow schooner condition, the *Alma* is again working. She is a teacher now, instructing young would-be mariners in the traditions of the sea. She is the only vessel in the Park that is completely operational.

Several of the old ferries may still be seen around the Bay, but no other is as superbly representative of the once grand fleet as the *Eureka*. Once the largest passenger ferry in the world, the *Eureka* was the last walking beam side-wheeler in commercial use in the United States when she retired in 1957. She could carry 2,300 people on her upper decks and 120 automobiles on her main deck. The *Eureka* also boasted underway entertainment in the form of nickelodeons and a magazine/sundries shop. If neither of those things appealed, you could stroll out onto the afterdeck and watch the Bay's maritime traffic in the bracing air.

Built in Tiburon in 1890, the double-ended, wooden-hulled *Eureka* began her career as the *Ukiah*, a combination railway car and passenger ferry. For thirty years she traveled between Tiburon and San Francisco. Then, in 1920, she went into the yard for extensive

conversion. Two years later, she emerged as the *Eureka*, and was used between Sausalito and San Francisco. In her nineteen years on the Sausalito run she frequently found herself in the same berth that she now occupies at the Hyde Street Pier. In 1941 she was transferred to the Southern Pacific Railroad route between the Oakland Mole and the San Francisco Ferry Building. Southern Pacific had her completely overhauled in 1954, but ferry service was already on the decline. When she sheared a massive crank pin in 1957 the Railroad could not economically justify repairs and she was permanently retired. With the retirement of the *Eureka*, transbay ferry service disappeared until 1971, when the Golden Gate Bridge District reinitiated a Sausalito ferry.

The heart of the ferry was her massive, vertical, 65-inch diameter cylinder with a single steam-driven piston. The power of each 12-foot stroke of the piston was sent up to the teeter-totter-like walking beam, then down to the 27-foot paddle wheel. To the delight of young and old, strategically placed windows made most of the *Eureka's* marvelous machinery visible to her passengers.

Everything about the *Eureka* seems to say that she is only waiting for word from her Captain to spring into action. Her machinery is greased and ready to go. Her main deck is crowded with vintage cars and trucks anxious for her to leave. Time has frozen for this great lady, but she still transports people — back to an age well worth visiting.

Wapama

US/ 1915/ 951 gt/ 205 ft/
40 ft/ 18 ft/ 850 hp/ 10 kts/wood

Steam began to replace sail in coastal shipping before the turn of the century. At first the steamships also carried sails, and were called steam schooners. By the time the *Wapama* was built, sails had all but disappeared from new steamships. Only the steam schooner name remained. The *Wapama* is a typically single-ended steam schooner with her pilothouse and passenger accommodations aft. The two masts at either end of the cargo deck have never felt the tug of canvas. As on modern cargo ships, the masts act as uprights for her long cargo booms. Power for her single, four-bladed screw came from a huge 850-horsepower triple-expansion steam engine. The engine is so massive for the horsepower delivered that it's not hard to understand why diesels replaced piston steam engines.

But the thing that is most impressive about the *Wapama* is not her steam engine or her serviceable Douglas fir hull. It's the elegance of her passenger accommodations. The individual cabins where the passengers slept are modest to say the least, but where the passengers gathered together the builder seems to have spared no expense. The lounge is a combination of rich oak paneling and red leather seating accented by brightly polished brass rails. A graceful curving staircase connects the lounge with a large, comfortable dining saloon below. The crew's dining area and day room aft

97

C. A. Thayer

*US/ 1895/ 452 gt/ 156 ft/
36 ft/ 19 ft*

of the passenger saloon is more spartan, but still a far cry from the steamy forecastle of the Cape Horners.

The *Wapama* was built in Oregon in 1915 and, like the *Thayer*, began her working life in the lumber trade along the North Coast. The steam schooners were ideal for getting in and out of the "dog hole" ports with their cliffside mills, coves so small that sailors said a dog couldn't turn around in them. Under her second owners she was used for general cargo and passengers between San Francisco and San Pedro. Just before World War II she was sold again and shifted to Alaska/Puget Sound duty. The *Wapama* worked actively through the war years, but by 1947 no one knew what to do with a small steam schooner and she was sold for scrap. She languished in the scrap heap until 1958, when the State of California rescued her and returned her to the Bay for restoration.

Ships don't begin their lives by being designed for a historical museum. Most of them, even the glamorous individuals, are dedicated to earning their living in an arduous life at sea. How then does a ship find itself securely tied to a pier and filled with chattering voices of another age, another life?

The *C. A. Thayer* began her life as a lumber schooner. She was well made by Hans Bendixsen from the fine Douglas fir that grew around his Humboldt Bay yard, but she wasn't particularly special. Her "bald-headed" rig without topsails left no hope of speed and, while she could carry more lumber than many contemporary three-masters, her capacity was small compared to the four- and five-masters of her day. She carried lumber for only seventeen years before a North Coast storm opened her seams and her owners decided she was not worth repairing when compared to a steam schooner. But ships like the *Thayer* don't die easily. There's always someone who thinks they have life left in them. For the *Thayer* it was thirteen years in the Alaskan salt-salmon trade. During World War I she even made trans-Pacific voyages to Australia and Hawaii, between fishing seasons.

By 1924 the salt-salmon business had fallen off and the *Thayer* found her decks loaded with steep-sided dories and a converted forward hold to berth forty fishermen. Now she was a codfisher, her hold filled with salt and smelly cod. She did well in the cod trade, but life in the Bering Sea was hard. In 1931 she was laid up and was out of service until 1942.

Another war had come, and the military decided that at least her hull was worth restoring as a barge. The Army did extensive work on her hull, then sent her to work off British Columbia and Alaska. Her masts were gone. Now she was towed everywhere she went, but she survived.

In 1956 the State of California, realizing that the *Thayer* was one of the last of the coastal schooners, decided she should be saved. She was pulled off the beach and, after some repairs, was sailed back to her San Francisco home.

Today the *Thayer* is special indeed. Not only is she among the last of the coastal lumber schooners, she is a link to a tradition of craftsmanship and seamanship that is hard to find today. Once an ordinary working ship, she is now a deservedly-recognized monument. She is a survivor.

In 1945 she was repurchased by her former cod fishing owner and fitted with makeshift masts. Again she set out into the freezing waters of the Bering Sea in search of cod. In 1950, when she made her last commercial voyage, she was the last sailing ship in commercial service on the Pacific Coast, but her time of glory had not yet come.

From cod fishing she went to a beach on Puget Sound where her unappreciative public was told she was a pirate ship.

Hercules

US/ 1907/ 414 gt/ 134.9 ft/
26.1 ft/ 15.5 ft/ 500 hp/ steel

There are two "Cape Horners" on the San Francisco waterfront, the *Balclutha* at Pier 43 and the less glamorous tug *Hercules* at the Hyde Street Pier. *Hercules*, with her sister ship *Goliah* in tow, rounded the Horn in 1907, driven by her then giant 1,000-horsepower triple-expansion steam engine. She was an ocean-going tug, a very important item in the final days of Pacific Coast sail where contrary winds made passages to northern ports difficult, long, and slow. Behind a tug the sailing ships could make the northern ports almost as quickly as the expanding fleet of steam schooners. The ocean tugs were also essential to getting out of the Bay against the prevailing westerlies. During her ocean-going days the *Hercules* also hauled log rafts down from the Pacific Northwest, and even worked on the Panama Canal.

In 1924 she was purchased by the Western Pacific Railroad for $62,500, a sizeable sum when inflated to present

(Photo by Paul Gordoner, courtesy of Santa Fe Railroad)

dollar value. Her pilothouse was raised, and for the next thirty-four years she hauled barges filled with railroad freight cars back and forth on the Bay. By 1957 she could no longer hold her own against smaller, more efficient diesel engines and, without ceremony or gold watch, she was retired from the railroad and active service.

In her ocean-going days the *Hercules* carried a crew of ten, nine to work the boat and one to cook. The crew stood watches of four hours on and eight off. One group of three worked the engine room, a second managed the deck and towing gear, and the third steered.

Pleasure Boats

There are all kinds of pleasure boaters on the Bay. Some go in for racing, some go on weekend cruises either up the Delta or to various anchorages around the Bay, some plan long cruises and spend months or years getting their boats ready for the ultimate trip, and some people have boats they almost never use. There is a kind of boat to suit nearly every person, and all of them can be seen on the Bay at one time or another. Weekends are of course the time to see pleasure boats on the water, but there are two really big days when more boats can be seen than any other time. In the spring there is Opening Day of Yachting Season, the last Sunday in April. Opening Day is like an Easter Parade of boats. More than thirty thousand "promenade" on the Bay in that one day. There is a semiorganized boat parade along the San Francisco waterfront, with many boats decorated to the theme of the year and prizes awarded to the best efforts. On Opening Day, boaters can have their boats blessed by clergymen aboard a Navy ship anchored in Raccoon Strait. The other big boating day is Labor Day in the fall. On both days, boats can be seen in large numbers everywhere. Many boaters visit other marinas in the evenings, and others anchor out for the day at various places around the Bay.

Pleasure boat hulls may be constructed of wood, steel, aluminum, fiberglass, or ferrocement. Most newer boats are fiberglass, because it lends itself to inexpensive mass production, is strong for its weight, and is one of the easiest hull materials to maintain in and out of the water. Most older boats and some larger contemporary boats have hulls fashioned from wood planking, wood strips, or plywood. Wood has been the traditional boat material because it was strong and plentiful, and boat builders knew how to use it. Wood, however, rots, is eaten by shipworms, and must be carefully maintained. Wooden boat construction is also more expensive than it used to be. Steel, because of its weight and required maintenance, is limited to larger boats where the owner wants to be assured of great strength. At the other end of the weight scale, aluminum is very expensive and therefore its use is limited to fast racing boats and some specialized commercial vessels. Ferrocement, which is the result of impregnating molded iron rod and wire with concrete, is a popular hull material with amateur boat builders. Interminable, painstaking hours go into each ferrocement hull before it's launched, making ferrocement boats a noble achievement in perseverance, and often in boatbuilding skill as well. Each hull material has its dogmatic defenders and detractors, and discussions of their relative merits can be quite lively.

Sailboats

Sailboats are easy to tell apart once you know what to look for. First, look at the number of masts. Second, look at their relative heights and where they are in relation to the tiller and bow. If the sails are up, look at their shape and how they are placed. If the sails are down check the forward stays, the wire ropes from the mast to the bow, to see if there is one or two, and look at the horizontal boom to see if there is a *gaff*, or second spar, resting on it.

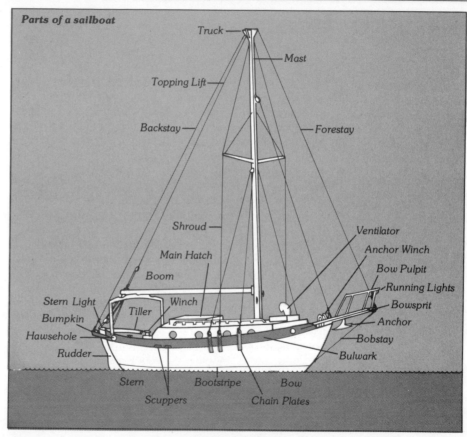

Parts of a sailboat

Truck — Mast — Topping Lift — Backstay — Forestay — Shroud — Ventilator — Main Hatch — Anchor Winch — Bow Pulpit — Boom — Running Lights — Stern Light — Winch — Bowsprit — Bumpkin — Tiller — Anchor — Hawsehole — Bobstay — Rudder — Bulwark — Stern — Bootstripe — Bow — Scuppers — Chain Plates

Sailboat Keels

The underwater profile of a sailboat determines some of its handling characteristics and therefore is related to what the boat is used for. A full keel makes for stability and the tendency to stay steady on a course. These are good cruising characteristics since the helmsman doesn't have to steer all the time. A well-balanced boat will sometimes sail herself for hours in a steady wind. Conversely, a full-keeled boat needs a larger turning radius and is therefore more difficult to maneuver in tight places. Fin-keeled boats are the opposite. They are quite sensitive and can turn on the proverbial dime. Fin keels are often used on quick, agile racers. Boats with cut-away keels fall somewhere in between. Daggerboard and centerboard keels that can be raised or lowered are also useful in racing, they can be raised to reduce

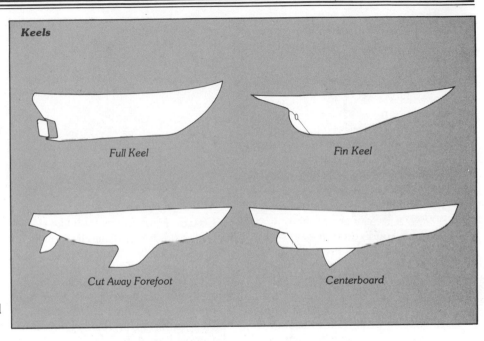

Keels

Full Keel

Fin Keel

Cut Away Forefoot

Centerboard

the wetted surface and drag when sailing downwind. They are likewise useful for sailing in shallow water because they can be partly raised to reduce the draft of the sailboat.

103

One Mast

Sloop

Sloop. Most of the one-masted boats on the Bay are sloops or cutters with *marconi*, or tall, triangular sails. Sloops fly two sails, a jib forward of the mast and a mainsail aft and fixed to the mast. In light air or when racing they may get extra power by using a brightly colored parachute-like sail called a spinnaker. Spinnakers are so colorful they look like rainbows, but don't be deceived by their beauty. They're tricky sails to use, and sailors who use them well are masters. If the boat appears to be using two spinnakers the forward one, using only lines to control it, is called a blooper. The spinnaker is held out to one side or the other with a pole, appropriately termed a spinnaker pole.

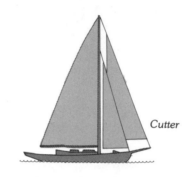

Cutter

Cutter. Most cutters look like sloops with an extra forward sail. If the sails are down, look for two wire rope stays in front of the mast. The forestay connecting the mast to the tip of the bow holds the foresail. The headstay connects a higher point on the mast with the bowsprit and holds a jib. Sloops normally have only one single headstay.

A cutter also has the mast stepped farther aft (two-fifths or more of the waterline length aft) than a sloop. A few boats that have only one headsail are still classed as cutters because of the position of the mast and the relative area of the sails it can carry. There are even some sloops, called double headsail sloops, that have two or more headsails. In the vast majority of the cases on the Bay, however, you can count on a boat with a single headsail being a sloop and one with two or more being a cutter.

Catboat

Catboat. Catboats have only one sail, and the mast is very close to the bow. Most catboats are small, some only ten feet long, but they may be larger. Many sailing dinghies used as tenders for larger boats are catboat rigged.

Two Masts

A boat with two masts may be a ketch, yawl, schooner, or junk. The majority of those on the Bay are ketches. Two-masted or split rigs are popular on larger boats, especially those over 40 feet, because they can have a large sail area while keeping the individual sails small enough to handle easily.

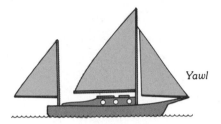

Yawl

Ketches and Yawls. In ketches and yawls the forward mast is taller than the after mast. The forward mast is called the mainmast, and the sail fixed to it the mainsail. The after mast is referred to as the mizzenmast, and its sail the mizzensail. Yawls tend to have small mizzensails relative to the other sails, and the mizzenmast is stepped well aft, behind the rudder post. Ketch masts are usually closer in size, and the mizzenmast is stepped forward of the rudder post. The general placement of the masts in relation to the whole hull is the best indication of which kind of boat you are looking at. Ketch masts always look more central, and yawl mizzens seem like afterthoughts.

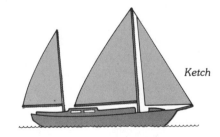

Ketch

Schooners. Schooners have two or more masts, with the foremast shorter than the mainmast. Once common in both working and racing fleets, the schooner rig is now relatively little used. A schooner can put more canvas aloft than a ketch of the same mast height, but the sails are often more difficult to handle.

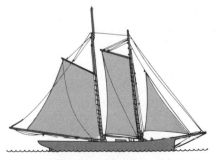

Schooner (Gaff Rigged)

105

Gaff Rigs

"Gaff rig" refers to the shape of the sails used. The gaff sail is trapezoidal in shape, and has a wood spar called a gaff at the top. Both single and multimasted vessels can be gaff-rigged. Sometimes all of the masted sails have gaffs, and sometimes only the mainsail is gaff-headed, while the other sails are triangular marconi sails.

The gaff rig is a traditional design that has long been used for fishing and work boats. It's a reliable rig but heavy because of the extra weight of the gaff. It can't sail as close to the wind as a marconi-rigged boat, but comes into its own downwind or on a reach (across the wind). They are especially good for cruising.

Few new boats are built with gaff rigs, but many people still like them for their traditional flavor. A number of people building their own boats choose this rig for its cruising ability.

Other Rigs

There are a number of Chinese junks on the Bay. These distinctive vessels have lug sails with full battens: horizontal wood or plastic strips that stiffen the sail. Lateen rigs common to the Nile Delta and the Persian Gulf are occasionally seen on the Bay. Once the lateen-rigged felucca was the most common fishing boat on San Francisco Bay (see chapter on fishing boats).

Multihulls

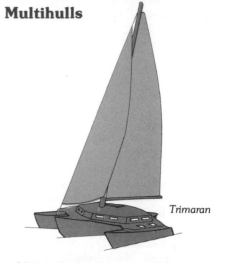

Trimaran

Multihulled sailboats are the major exception to the rule that sailboats have displacement hulls. These shallow-draft vessels can often plane quite well, and consequently most are extremely fast. In addition, they have great initial stability because their weight is spread out over a wide area. This stability allows more sail area to be carried in higher winds than would be safe on a monohull.

Multihull boats generally do not have a keel. They gain directional stability by

Motorsailers

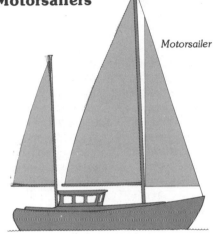

Motorsailer

hull shape and/or by center or dagger-boards. Because there is no heavy weight built into the hull, these boats generally can't sink.

Although multihulls have great stability, they can be flipped over under certain wind and sea conditions. They are then equally stable upside down and consequently difficult to right. Experimentation with various new designs has made modern multihulls safer, and people have crossed all of the world's oceans in them. Many people consider them to be ideal cruising boats. Because they don't heel over to any significant degree, things inside the boat don't slide around much and life can be lived on the level. In addition, the large deck makes them ideal for warm, sunny climates.

One thing you will discover if you mention multihulls is that everyone has a strong opinion and there is no middle ground. Perfect strangers will accost you on the street to share their point of view.

The motorsailer is an attempt to combine the best aspects of both sail and power boats in a single vessel. They have enough fuel and horsepower to perform well under power alone when necessary, and sufficient sail to proceed under the power of the wind when that is desirable. Motorsailers are compromises, but some of them are quite successful.

Some motorsailers are easily distinguished. They have a large mast or masts, can carry plenty of sail, and also have an enclosed cockpit or wheelhouse for motoring with the helmsman out of the weather. Other motorsailers are more difficult to identify. They look basically like any other sailboat, but hidden from view is a powerful engine, usually a diesel, and an abundance of fuel. Most motorsailers fall somewhere in between. Some of the newer ones can be spotted because they have big windows on the forward side of the cabin. This may not be a wheelhouse at all, but a large and sunny saloon. The engine that comes with this type of yacht is usually large and powerful.

Power

Engines for pleasure boats are either gasoline or diesel-powered. Gasoline engines are lighter in weight, cheaper, and can produce a higher speed faster than can a diesel. They are generally limited to smaller boats of all kinds, and to medium-sized boats looking for sprightly performance. Their light weight and lower initial cost make them the choice of many people, especially for boats under 30 feet. Gas is explosive, however, and special blowers, venting, and other safety precautions must be taken on boats using gas engines.

Diesel engines are larger, heavier, and more expensive to buy. Horsepower for horsepower they are a larger investment than are gasoline engines. Conversely, they use less fuel to maintain a given speed, and diesel fuel is cheaper than gasoline. Boats with diesel engines tend to be larger, cruising types. Diesel fuel is far less explosive than gasoline, and many people prefer it because it is safer.

Modern technology is creating smaller, lighter diesels, and there are even diesel outboards available, but they are more expensive than gasoline engines.

One major difference between the engines found on boats and those found in cars, trucks, and motorcycles is the method used for cooling them. Marine engines are water cooled, and the water is drawn directly from the ocean, bay, or lake the boat is sailing on. Salt water is corrosive, however, and salt deposits can interfere with cooling efficiency. Marine engines used in salt water generally use recirculating fresh water for cooling the engine, with salt water pumped in from outside to cool the fresh water. The heat is removed in a heat exchanger where hot water from the engine passes close to cold water from outside, which absorbs the heat and is then pumped overboard.

Most boats with engines are propeller driven, but in recent years water jet drive has become popular. Essentially the water jet is a high speed water pump that sucks water from a low point in the hull and shoots it out the stern. Steering is accomplished by turning the water jet, so no rudders are needed. Reverse is a cup that drops into the exiting stream, reversing the direction of its thrust. The water jets are fast and safe. but the high pump speeds generally require a gasoline engine.

Boat hulls are grouped in two general categories, regardless of the materials in them. Those that can achieve greater speed by partially or completely rising out of the water are said to have *planing hulls*. The ideal planing hull is flat and glides over the surface of the water. Flat bottoms have a tendency to pound uncomfortably, however, on any water rougher than a calm inland lake. The compromise that retains speed while not

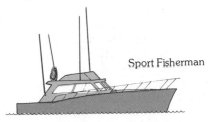

Express

Sport Fisherman

pounding is a semiplaning hull with a deep "V" shape forward, gradually shifting to a flatter profile at the stern. With the addition of small ribs or shelves along the length of the hull, called *strakes*, the semiplaning hull can behave quite well under most conditions.

The second hull group consists of those that, by virtue of their shape and construction, are incapable of rising out of the water under most circumstances. Such hulls always displace a volume of water equal in weight to the weight of the entire boat and its contents. Because of this they are called displacement hulls. Most boats have displacement hulls, including all the keeled sailboats, heavy powerboats, rowboats, and most commercial boats.

Powerboat Types

The types of powerboats are not nearly as distinct as are sailboat types. There are few hard and fast rules; one type just seems to shade into another. Part of the confusion arises out of geographical differences in definition, and part from the fact that the manufacturers themselves transpose terms for sales appeal. Whatever its origin, the confusion can make telling the various powerboats apart like trying to distinguish the various models of Detroit cars.

Still, there are differences between powerboats, as the ads in the newspapers and magazines will tell you. The categories used here are the ones most commonly used by Bay Area boat brokers. It should be remembered that they are general cases. Combinations of different characters allow the manufacturer to name his vessel pretty much as he chooses. One further note: many of these boats have canvas enclosures for the afterdeck, cockpit, or even the flying bridge. To distinguish the true lines of a powerboat you must ignore the canvas.

Express. These boats tend to be on the smaller end of the scale. The steering station is more or less amidships, and is open to the cockpit aft. The steering station usually has two built-in seats for the skipper and mate. An express may have a flying bridge, but often doesn't.

Sport Fisherman. An enclosed interior wheelhouse and flying bridge help to distinguish these boats. They tend to have large cockpits with low freeboard for ease in landing fish. Many have a life rail around the stern. The flying bridge is usually farther aft than the bridge on a sedan so the helmsman can

Convertible

see how the fishermen are doing and respond accordingly. A sport fisherman that is actually used for fishing will look spiky with fishing poles and gear.

Sedan

Sedan. The sedan has an enclosed wheelhouse like the sport fisherman, but tends to have more cabin room, leaving a smaller afterdeck. The freeboard is greater around the afterdeck and generally they don't carry fixed fishing gear. Sedans may not have a flying bridge. If there is one, it tends to be farther forward than one on a sport fisherman. Sometimes the flying bridge has a hard top, called, naturally, a hardtop/flying bridge.

Convertible. Convertibles are a compromise between an express and a sport fisherman (or sedan, depending on the builder). Their most distinctive feature is the large double, folding or sliding doors between the cockpit and the enclosed wheelhouse. Like the top on a convertible car, these doors can be secured open to join the wheelhouse with the cockpit.

Tri-Cabin

Tri-Cabin. Three cabins on a split-level layout distinguish these boats. The main cabin sits higher than the fore and aft cabins, and contains an inside steer-ing station. There may be a flying bridge over the main cabin. If the outside steer-ing station is over the aft cabin, it's called a raised-deck tri-cabin.

Trawler

Trawler. These pleasure boats are loosely modeled after the tried-and-true fishing trawlers. Their most distinguishing feature is the full displacement hull, which gives them added comfort and stability for offshore cruising. The bow is much less raked than in other power-boats, and the wheelhouse/main cabin windows are larger. Over all there is a less streamlined look to trawlers. Many trawlers have large, roomy flying bridges.

Where to Watch Boats

San Francisco

No matter how long you watch boats on the Bay, there's still a thrill to seeing a big merchant or bobbing fisherman come in from sea. Columbus may have proven that the horizon is not a sheer cliff, but there's still mystery about what lies beyond what the eye can see. Those who emerge through the shroud of fog or inch up over the horizon as they make for the Golden Gate are returning from King Neptune's fabled world.

Any place along San Francisco's western coastline is good for watching seafarers return from the mighty Pacific. It's all public property and doesn't cost a cent to use. The only requirements for its enjoyment are enthusiasm and, occasionally, warm clothes. By bicycle, horse, foot, or roller skate you can travel on or beside more than four miles of beach uninterrupted by even a single hot dog stand, while the roar of the Pacific surf erases all images of the City.

(A) The Cliff House

This is The Place to watch boats, sea lions, sea birds, and fantastic sunsets, or to play an old nickelodeon. On clear, cold days the Farallon Islands, 28 miles offshore, seem almost close enough to touch. Once, Emperor Norton proposed building a bridge from this site to the Farallons — what for, only he knew.

(B) USS San Francisco Monument

The monument and its parking lot command a spectacular view of the Golden Gate, the Farallon Islands, and the Marin headlands. Immediately offshore to the north, Mile Rock Light marks the southern side of the Gate. Mile Rock Light has been automated; its flattened top is used to land helicopters when the light needs servicing. The white buildings across the channel are the Point Bonita Light Coast Guard Station, which marks the north side of the Gate.

(C) Fort Point

Nestled under the southern end of the Golden Gate Bridge, this fort was the guard post before the Civil War. Regular tours are conducted through this National Historic Site. The nearby rock-walled waterfront is much used by fishermen, especially during the striped bass season, and provides the closest possible view of passing ships.

Directly above the fort is a parking lot and observation area maintained by the Golden Gate Bridge District. This is the place to park if you should plan to walk across the Bridge, something everyone should do at least once. Short of hiring a helicopter, a bridge walk is the best way to look directly down on passing boats.

A pathway extends eastward from Fort Point along the shoreline to the historic ships at the Hyde Street Pier. The walk is less than four miles, but so full of things to stop and look at, it's hard to do in one day.

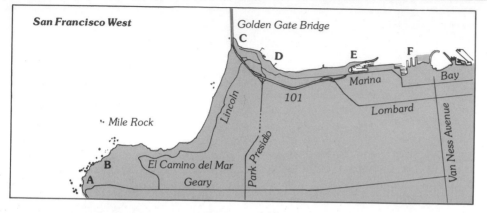

San Francisco West

Golden Gate Bridge

C

D

E

F

Marina

Bay

101

Lombard

Lincoln

Park Presidio

Van Ness Avenue

Mile Rock

B

El Camino del Mar

A

Geary

(D) Coast Guard Station, Fort Point

While the station is not open to the public for the same reasons that fire stations are generally not open to the public, it is easily seen from the path. The station and its patrol boats are fairly typical of Coast Guard Search and Rescue outposts. There are enough people at the station to man one or two boats twenty-four hours a day. Whether towing stricken craft or pulling people out of the water, the search and rescue boats respond to all calls of distress on or in the water.

(E) St. Francis Yacht Club

The recently rebuilt yacht club is impressive, but the things to look at here are the yachts. Lined up along the north and west walls are some of the most impressive sail and motor yachts on the Bay. Those who walk out on the breakwater may see a scow schooner like that sailed by Joshua Slocum on his solo trip around the world, as well as an old German steam-powered police patrol boat. From the end of the breakwater you can watch wind surfers bravely scoot to Sausalito and back.

(F) Fort Mason

Fort Mason used to be the headquarters of the Military Sea Transportation Service, and is now the headquarters of the Golden Gate National Recreation Area. The National Park Service has only recently taken possession of the fort, and it's not completely developed. It is worth checking here to see what's currently happening on the Park's vast public waterfront.

(G) Maritime Museum

From a distance, the Maritime Museum overlooking Aquatic Park looks like the bridge and superstructure of a great merchant ship. Inside is a marvelous collection of pieces from old ships, together with photographs that help visitors develop a sense of the old ships. There are also collections of ship models, scrimshaw from the heyday of whaling, and a tiny sailboat built by a young Japanese man who crossed the Pacific in it single-handed. Don't miss the panoramic photographs showing the chaos of San Francisco Bay during the age of windjammers. The Museum is on Beach Street, one block west from the end of the Hyde Street Cable Car line.

(H) National Historic Ships, Hyde Street Pier

Have you ever wondered what sea duty was like at the turn of the century? Step aboard the *Thayer* — that's when she was carrying lumber along the Pacific Coast. How about ferries in the twenties, did you ever dream about commuting when things were slower? Try the *Eureka*. In the twenties she was the largest passenger ferry in the world. If neither of these ships appeal, or if you want more, step aboard the steam schooner *Wapama* or cast your eyes on the tug *Hercules* and the hay scow *Alma*. Don't let the fact that it's free deter you, the National Historic Ships are so rich

you can never take them in completely. Parking in the vicinity is difficult, so treat yourself to a ride on the Hyde Street Cable Car.

(I) Fisherman's Wharf

This is the perennial boatwatcher's Mecca. Where else can you see fishing boats, Harbor Tours boats, a Cape Horn schooner, paddle-wheeled tug, water taxi, and modern oil spill container? Should you grow tired of walking, there is a helicopter that will take you up for a change of perspective. Fisherman's Wharf also means food, seafood in great abundance. Whether a sidewalk cocktail or a sit-down affair with fine linen, the fare is unbeatable. The Franciscan indulges the curiosity of its customers by announcing the arriving and departing ships as they pass. If you have always harbored a secret desire to visit a federal prison, Fisherman's Wharf has that too. Catch the Harbor Tours boat to Alcatraz

and see where Al Capone spent his time. Remember, though, that the prison has become quite popular since they gave up locking the cells. Reservations are required.

If a visit to prison seems a bit threatening, then walk out to the vista pier on the Bay side of the Franciscan Restaurant. Benches and telescopes out over the water make this the perfect spot for the insatiable boatwatcher.

West on Jefferson Street is the City's famous fishing fleet. The piers are open and the public is welcome to wander out for a close look at the boats. Most of the boats in the inner basin are sport fishing party boats or commercial salmon boats, plus a few long liners. Slightly farther west, out by Scoma's Restaurant, is a second group of fishing boats, many larger than those in the inner basin. Special note: At the end of the street behind Scoma's is the Fisherman's Wharf Seafood Company. They are primarily

113

wholesalers, but live Maine lobsters and other sea food can be purchased by occasional walk-in customers.

No visit to Fisherman's Wharf is complete without boarding the *Balclutha*, San Francisco's own full-rigged Cape Horner. Full-rigged ships like this are extremely rare today, but they were once the backbone of every nation's merchant fleet. Of those remaining, the resident *Balclutha* is a gem. She is maintained by the Maritime Museum as a vibrant floating museum, telling her story of the last great days of sail to thousands of visitors annually.

(39) Pier 39

San Francisco's newest waterfront attraction is Pier 39, the large shopping center/restaurant complex. Marinas on both sides are filled with sail, power, and charter boats. The south side boasts a good view of the passenger terminal at Pier 35. A carousel, a penny arcade, high

divers, and almost endless Bay views are the highlights, but by no means all there is to be seen. Quick visits have a way of stimulating a desire for more.

(35) Pier 35

Pier 35 is the passenger terminal for the Bay. Cruise ships come in here regularly. If they tie up on the west side of the pier they can be easily seen from Pier 39 or from the Embarcadero. Most of the cruise lines permit visitors on their ships when they are docked. The times and numbers of visitors permitted varies from line to line, but because cruise ships calling in San Francisco are foreign flag vessels, pemits are required before boarding. It is advisable to check with the individual line several weeks ahead of time to get a boarding pass. Sometimes your travel agent can arrange for you to visit a cruise ship.

(31-33) Piers 31 and 33

Between Piers 31 and 33 Greenpeace, the environmental organization dedicated to stopping the killing of whales and other marine mammals, frequently has one of their ships open for public tours. From these mother ships, the environmentalists go out in rubber boats with outboard motors and place themselves between the whalers and their prey.

(19, 23, 27) Piers 19, 23, and 27

These three piers regularly receive traditional break-bulk cargo ships. Each affords a good view of break-bulk cargo handling from the Embarcadero. Pier 27 often handles large agricultural, earth moving, and mining equipment.

(9) Pier 9

Pier 9 is the center of tug boat and water taxi service on the Bay. Brown and black water taxis, blue and white pilot launches, and orange and white tugs line the north side of the pier. The huge red and white barge at Pier 15 carries paper products from Canada. The south side of Pier 9 is filled with different tugs and tow boats from the various Red Stack fleets.

(7-9) Between Piers 7 and 9

This small pier behind the Waterfront Restaurant belongs to the San Francisco Bar Pilots, the men who take merchant ships in and out of the Golden Gate. One or two of their pilot boats are generally tied up here, while the third is always on station eleven miles outside the Gate. The pilot boats come alongside the moving merchant ship and the pilot boards by climbing a ladder up the side of the ship. The Bar Pilot boats are all white with blue trim and orange cabin tops. On either side, in blue block letters, is the word "PILOT."

(7) Pier 7

Pier 7 is a parking lot, but is open to pedestrian traffic as well. It is a good place to watch tugs and water taxis coming and going. Looking south from Pier 7 you can see the ferryboat *Klamath* permanently tied up at Pier 5. Pier 7 also has a good view of the Bay, Treasure Island, the Bay Bridge, and the upper part of Anchorage 9.

(J) Ferry Building

The Ferry Building is one of the few buildings on the waterfront to survive the earthquake and fire of 1906. Today the north wing houses the World Trade Center, with offices for many of the international businesses associated with the Bay. The south wing contains the offices of the Port of San Francisco and other government agencies. The second floor houses the mineral museum of the California Bureau of Mines and Geology, with mineral samples from every county in the state, as well as amazingly large gold nuggets that could tempt anyone to give up boat watching for a gold pan and a burro.

Behind the Ferry Building is the new Golden Gate Ferry landing, with an observation platform. Ferry riding is a special treat, and one of the easiest and cheapest ways to boat watch. There is a feeling of calm when riding on a ferry, even during the heaviest commute hours. Somehow the ferries mean gaiety, a feeling that captivates all who ride on them. Perhaps it's their link to the past or their association with the ocean.

(22½) Fireboat *Phoenix*

Just north of the Bay Bridge, at the foot of Harrison Street, is Engine Company Number 1, the home of the *Phoenix*, San Francisco's full-time fireboat. Fires are a major problem in any port. Often they can be fought only from the water. The *Phoenix* can best be admired from the Embarcadero.

115

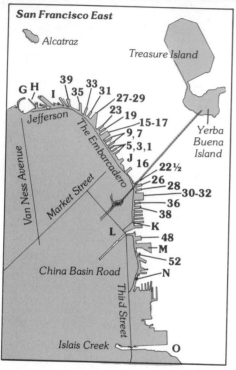

San Francisco East

Alcatraz

Treasure Island

G H **39** **33** **31**
I **35** **27-29**
23 **19**
Jefferson **15-17**
The Embarcadero **9,7**
5,3,1
Yerba
Buena
Island
J **16**
22½
Van Ness Avenue
26 **28**
Market Street
30-32
36
38
L **K**
48
China Basin Road **M**
52
N
Third Street
Islais Creek **O**

(30,32) Piers 30 and 32

These integrated piers are the home of Delta Lines and their passenger/cargo

liners, the four *Santas*. Delta allows a limited amount of visiting on their passenger ships when they are in port. Passes are not required, but check with Delta about visiting hours and remember that for safety the number of visitors permitted aboard is limited. Delta's break-bulk ships also call at these piers, and can be seen from the Embarcadero.

(36, 38) Piers 36 and 38

Both of these piers are in-water shipyards that specialize in light ship repair that doesn't require dry docking. Deck operations and exterior painting are easily seen from the Embarcadero. This is a good place to check periodically, because of the variety of ships worked on.

(K) *Dolphin P. Rempp*

This fine old coastal steam schooner, now a restaurant, is entered from below her former waterline. Built at the time that shipping was making the transition

from sail to steam, she still carries three masts and rigging for sails.

(L) China Basin

No two visits to China Basin are the same. The collection of ships and boats is constantly changing but always interesting. From fairy-tale yard tugs to giant merchant ships, there is more variety here than any other place on the Bay. Plan to walk the Third Street drawbridge, which is still operating. With any luck, they will open the bridge while you're there.

(48) Pier 48

This pier is used exclusively by Crown-Zellerbach to receive paper products and lumber from British Columbia. The ships that call here are unique "neo-bulk" carriers that were built specifically to carry paper and lumber. Their gantry cranes can lift eight large rolls of newsprint at a time.

Oakland

(M) Mission Rock Terminal

This big terminal can handle six ships at a time. It's used by both conventional and containerized cargo carriers. The parking lot between it and Pier 48 to the north affords the best view of loading and unloading operations. Pacific Telephone and Telegraph keeps a cable-tending barge and its tug next to the parking lot. Judging by the number of people with lines in the water, fishing is pretty good here as well.

(52) Pier 52

Pier 52 is the San Francisco home of the last operating railroad tug on the Bay. Up to six times a day the *Paul P. Hastings* and its barge makes the trip between here and the Santa Fe Railroad yards in Richmond. Docking maneuvers, loading, and unloading are easily seen from China Basin Street. This is a great place to watch a seldom-seen part of railroad operations.

(N) Agua Vista Park

This modest park and its fishing pier offer the best view of a working shipyard on the Bay. Bethlehem Steel's floating dry docks are always busy with repairs and major conversions. Both military and merchant ships use the yard. Pier 70, on the Bay side of Bethlehem, is hidden by the shipyard, but the strange-looking automobile carriers that tie up there can be seen from the park as they dock. The tankers in the distance are anchored in Anchorage 9, where they discharge some of their crude oil cargo to other tankers or barges. This operation is necessary for the huge tankers to reduce their draft to get to the refineries in the shallower northern Bay.

(O) Islais Creek Channel

There are tiny parks for public boat watching on both sides of the drawbridge across the channel. The drawbridge is necessary to let bulk liquid tankers into the upstream terminal.

(A) Portview Park

At the western end of Seventh Street, this pocket park offers the best possible view of the South Bay, Oakland Outer Harbor, the Naval Supply Center, and the entrance to the Oakland/Alameda Estuary. The park has something for everyone: picnic tables, fishing pier, snack bar, restrooms, and a three-story viewing platform overlooking the port. From the platform you have the very best view of a working container terminal in the Bay Area. Should you tire of boat watching, in the opposite direction are Alameda Naval Air Station's busy runways. In the Air Station's foreground, the Estuary is always busy with ships and boats of all sizes. The park is always open, but the viewing platform is closed at night.

(B) Middle Harbor Park

This park is hard to find but worth the effort. Take Ferro Street off Middle

117

Harbor Road at the United States Lines. The last quarter mile is one-lane. The park is quite small but is landscaped, has a fishing pier, and is on the shore of the Estuary. Best of all, the park commands a great view of a modern container terminal. Across the Estuary is Alameda Naval Air Station, east of which is Todd Shipyard's giant floating dry dock. The park does not have restrooms.

(C) Jack London Square

Jack London Square is named after one of Oakland's most famous former residents. The story goes that London was an oyster pirate working out of this area when he was young. He was befriended by a bartender who encouraged him to study and write. The young pirate became so fascinated by words that he made them his life. Many of the characters in his novels were drawn from people he met on the Oakland waterfront. Heinhold's First and Last Chance Bar, where the hard-drinking novelist's life changed direction, is still in business at the Square near London's restored Alaskan log cabin.

Don't be in a hurry at Jack London Square. There's more than enough to keep a boat watcher busy for a couple of days. Aside from parking, it can all be done for free. Travel to the Orient on a passing cargo ship or up to Alaska on an old power yacht. Let your mind wander the globe. If you do feel like spending money, the restaurants and shops, both on the Square and in adjacent Jack London Village, have much to offer the musing mariner. (Special note: The Great Atlantic Lobster Company, west of the Square at the foot of Clay St., is mainly a wholesale outlet but sells to walk-in trade. Good fresh lobster.)

Do you want to see a fireboat close up? Look behind the fire house on the west end of the Square. There she is not ten feet away; the *City of Oakland*, grey and white with sparkling red fire-fighting equipment.

The marinas at Jack London Square have several classic motor yachts that alone make a visit worthwhile. Across the Estuary are the restaurants and marinas of Alameda's Mariner Square. The cement ramps east of Mariner Square were used to launch ships from a World War II shipyard. Frequently, 378-foot Coast Guard Cutters are tied up west of Mariner Square and, beyond the cutters but still in excellent view, is Todd Shipyards.

(D) Estuary Park

East of Jack London Square on Embarcadero Road, Estuary Park features picnic facilities for groups, guest docks for visiting boats, a launching ramp for small boats, and a fishing pier. It has the same Estuary view as Jack London Square, with one exception. To the east, about 50 yards from the guest docks, is

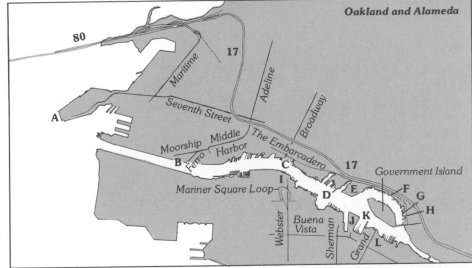

Oakland and Alameda

Merritt Shipyard. The structure on the southwest corner of the shipyard is a floating dry dock, which is flooded to receive a ship, then pumped out again to raise the ship out of the water. The shipyard is owned by Crowley Maritime Corporation, and is frequently used as a repair facility for their offshore tugs and barges.

(E) Ninth Avenue Terminal

Do not try to go into the terminal. The view is better from a restaurant parking lot northeast of the terminal, and it's far safer. Ninth Avenue is a bulk and break-bulk cargo terminal, and the ships that call here are both conventional, multi-craned break-bulk carriers, and bulk cargo carriers. Sometimes the ship's deck gear, rather than shoreside cranes, is used. It's fascinating to watch.

Across the channel is Government Island, a basic training center for the Coast Guard. At low tide the remnants of ship ribs jut out of the water offshore. They are all that remain of a fleet of sail ships operated by the Alaska Packers Association (see *Balclutha, Thayer*) as tenders for the salmon canneries.

The parking lot is also the beginning of Embarcadero Cove Marina, which has a good mix of modern sail and power boats, together with beautiful old classics.

(F) Pacific Dry Dock

Pacific Dry Dock is not a public facility. It's a working boatyard where only those with specific, legitimate business should venture. The reason for including it here is that boatwatchers can easily see through the fence from a safe distance. The view? Tugs. This is one of the maintenance yards for Crowley Maritime

119

Corporation's Red Stack tugs and Harbor Tours boats. If you ever wondered what a tug wears under its watery kilt, this is the place to satisfy your curiosity. Let your eyes wander around the yard. There are spare parts for many of the Bay's most active work boats. Having the spare parts available minimizes the amount of time a boat has to be out of service when something goes wrong. Look closely at the tug fenders lying in the yard. Off the boats it's clear that there is more to a tug fender than cut-up tires.

(G) Victoria Station/Quinn's Lighthouse

These restaurants overlook a pleasure boat marina, Government Island, and Oakland's fishing fleet. The walkways between the boats and the restaurants are public for your enjoyment.

(H) Dock Cafe

This wharf, known in the fleet as "Evans Radio Dock," is home to

Oakland's sizeable salmon and albacore fleet. Because of the limited dockside space, the boats "raft up" — several boats tie up next to each other with tires or fenders between them. Only one of the boats in a raft ties up to the pier. No one seems to mind having people cross their boat en route to the outside boats. If one of the boats has to leave and you're not there, no problem. The other skippers will move your boat with every bit as much care as you would move it yourself.

Alameda

(I) Mariner Square

Alameda's Mariner Square, on top of the tunnels under the Estuary, is synonymous with pleasure boats. Yacht brokers, chandlery, and restaurants are assembled around an impressively diverse collection of sail and power boats. This is a great place to test your skill at distinguishing one pleasure boat

from another. If you get stumped, you can watch merchant shipping or workboats on the Estuary.

(J) Encinal Terminal

This basin was once the home of the Alaska Packers Association and their large fleet of square and fore and aft rigged fishing ships. Today it is the largest privately-owned open steamship terminal in the United States. It's not open to the public, but several terminal operations can be easily viewed from the point where Sherman Street crosses the Alameda Belt Line Railroad. The terminal is primarily a bulk cargo facility handling a variety of cargos, including automobiles, lumber, and bulk liquids. The berth nearest Sherman Street can also handle containers.

(K) Alameda Yacht Harbor

Alameda Yacht Harbor is at the end of Entrance Road, tucked between a red brick warehouse and bulk liquid storage

Marin County

tanks. Don't be put off by the guard shack at the entrance to the yacht harbor; the frontage on the Estuary is a public access area. Just east of the yacht harbor is a tallow/corn syrup terminal frequently visited by Chinese and Japanese tankers. Across the Estuary is Oakland's Ninth Avenue bulk cargo terminal. The yacht harbor itself is filled with a delightful collection of classic and modern pleasure boats.

(L) Foot of Grand Street

This is a public boat-launching ramp actively used by small boat fishermen. West of the ramp, just beyond a fence, is the Harbor Tug and Barge yard, with its collection of harbor tugs and pusher boats. On the other side of the ramp is Alameda Marina. Look for the unique fireboat. Across the Estuary is the Coast Guard's basic training facility.

(A) Golden Gate National Recreation Area

This park has so many spectacular views of the Bay and of Marin County coast that it is impractical to try to list them. The park is a place for discoveries and exploration, both personal and of the outside world. The best way to see it is on foot, but bicycles and automobiles are also practical. Conzelman Road, west of the freeway, rewards those who don't suffer from acrophobia or timorousness on narrow, winding roads with one commanding view after another. When special ships arrive or depart, the road is jammed.

Muir Beach Overlook, off Highway 1, is an old coastal defense battery. The moods of the fog here make the views ever-changing and often mysterious. On clear days the overlook has a fine view of the northern shipping channel, the Farallon Islands and, at the right time of year, migrating Gray Whales.

(B) Vista Point

Day or night, this overlook is a must. It can only be reached by traveling north across the Golden Gate Bridge. When you first arrive the vista may be so large and the scenery so overpowering that nothing seems to be happening. Keep looking, and you will notice that the scene is not static. It's filled with little ships and boats that refuse to be painted in one place.

(C) Lime Point

On the east side of the Bridge off Conzelman Road is a dirt parking lot. The parking lot itself offers good boat watching. But for those who must get really close, a foot path leads out to Lime Point Light. Stay away from the rocks, the currents here are extremely treacherous. Every vessel entering or leaving the Bay must pass this point.

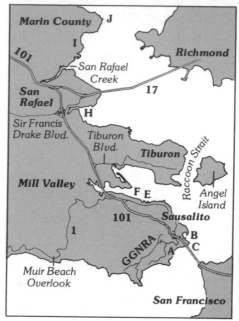

(D) Sausalito

For boatwatchers, Sausalito means yachts. Offshore from the Trident Restaurant on southern Bridgeway you may see an old Baltic Trader sailboat or an elegant motoryacht riding at anchor. The Sausalito waterfront is lined with marinas berthing boats both modest and grand. Behind the Post Office is Pelican Harbor, the largest assembly of traditional wood sailing boats on the Bay.

(E) Corps of Engineers Bay Model

Just off Bridgeway is the Army Corps of Engineers giant Bay Model and museum. The hydrologic model is used to study tides and currents in the Bay, and is open to the public. Behind the model building are the home piers for the Corps of Engineers dredge and Bay clean-up vessels. Going around the building on the south side takes you to the home of Sausalito's fishing fleet.

(F) Waldo Point

Waldo Point, on the northwest end of Sausalito, is a houseboat community. From thrown-together structures that seem barely habitable to multistory apartments, these floating residences carry on a Bay tradition that dates back to the Gold Rush. Waldo Point is the apparent final resting place for the ferries *Issaquah* and *Charles Van Damm*.

If you plan to visit Sausalito from San Francisco, think about taking the ferry.

(G) Tiburon

Tiburon is the jumping-off place for one of the commute ferries to San Francisco and for the ferry to Angel Island State Park. The Corinthian and San Francisco Yacht Clubs are nearby, and Raccoon Strait between Tiburon and Angel Island is a favorite haunt of Bay pleasure boaters, especially on weekends. On Opening Day of the yachting season, the last Sunday in April, a Navy ship anchors off the cove with clergymen aboard to bless passing boats.

(H) Larkspur Ferry Terminal

This space age terminal is the Marin County home of the "jet ferries," so

Richmond

called because of their unique water-jet drive. The space available to maneuver the ferries is quite restricted, but the skilled skippers make the job look easy. Sometimes it's easier to see the ferries maneuver from Sir Francis Drake Boulevard.

(I) Loch Lomond Marina

Loch Lomond Marina is a good place to watch weekend boat traffic in and out of San Rafael Channel. The best view is from the outer eastern breakwater. Fishing is reportedly fair from the breakwater as well.

(J) McNears Beach

The quarry south of the park supplies rock for breakwaters, jetties, and bank protection all over the Bay. Barges and their pusher tugs are frequently seen here. Occasionally you can also see a submarine en route to Mare Island.

(A) Point Molate Beach Park

Take the Point Molate exit from Highway 17 west. Just before the gate to the Navy Base, turn left. The park looks out at the Richmond/San Rafael Bridge, and is a good place to watch ships en route to and from river and North Bay ports. The Navy Base is a fuel storage facility for the many military operations on the Bay. Its pier, northwest of the park, is always busy receiving and dispatching fuel.

Stop on the hill as you return from the park. From here you can look over the bridge to Chevron's Long Wharf, one of the most active terminals on the Bay.

(B) Castro Point

Now the site of Redrock Marina, Castro Point was the eastern terminal for the Richmond/San Rafael Ferry until 1956. The present fishing pier and launching ramp are parts of the old ferry slips. Take a close look at the breakwater around the marina. It was made by

sinking old wooden barges, then filling them with rocks and debris.

(C) George Miller Jr. Park

Off Garrard Boulevard in Point Richmond, Miller Park is a good place to watch the operations at Chevron's Long Wharf. Binoculars are useful if you are curious about equipment details. Both crude and products tankers, often three at a time, can be seen here. In addition, bunkering barges operate regularly out of the inside of the Wharf.

The fishing pier at the end of Garrard Boulevard is a good place to watch ships move in and out of Richmond's port. It also has a good view of up-river ship traffic and of the Santa Fe barge operations.

(D) Canal Boulevard

Canal Boulevard is the main street through Richmond's western port facilities. There is a lot of truck traffic, so this is not a good place for casual gawking

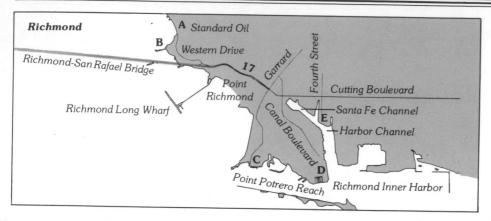

Map labels: Richmond; A Standard Oil; B; Western Drive; Richmond-San Rafael Bridge; 17; Garrard; Fourth Street; Point Richmond; Cutting Boulevard; Richmond Long Wharf; Santa Fe Channel; E; Harbor Channel; Canal Boulevard; C; D; Point Potrero Reach; Richmond Inner Harbor

North Bay

Vallejo

Vallejo is the home of the California Maritime Academy, which trains officers for the U.S. merchant fleet. Their training ship *Golden Bear* can be seen at its berth as you cross the Carquinez Bridge. The Academy's fine library is open to the public, and contains a broad selection of trade publications and books on all aspects of merchant shipping.

There are several places along the Vallejo waterfront where you can look across the narrow strait to Mare Island Naval Shipyard. Presently the base is used primarily for submarines. Both conventional diesel electric and nuclear powered boats call at Mare Island. A more elevated view of the base is possible from the Highway 37 bridge across the Napa River.

The marinas in Vallejo have many interesting power boats that provide a marvelous excuse for a casual stroll along the waterfront.

while driving. The terminal at the end of the street is operated by Pasha Truckway to receive foreign cars, and to ship a smaller number of U.S.-made cars. The auto processing is fun to watch if you don't plan to buy a car soon. Think about how much you want a particular engine, interior, and color in a car, and then try to imagine that desired car reaching you when it has to be shipped from here. Amazingly, the system works.

The next three docks up the harbor channel are oil products terminals. Products tankers and bunkering barges can frequently be seen. They are also used for fueling ships at the piers.

Across the channel from these facilities is Richmond's new containerized cargo terminal, scheduled to open in 1980.

(E) South Fourth Street

The terminal adjacent to Fourth Street is a typical bulk products facility. It's easy to look through the fence and watch the cranes gracefully handle cargo. At the head of the same channel is the headquarters of Western Tug, and the biggest tow boat on the Bay.

Crockett

Just east of the Carquinez Bridge is the C&H Sugar plant. Molasses is brought in by ship from Hawaii and converted to sugar here. Both ships and barges are used to bring the molasses to the plant. Another smaller ship takes bagged sugar from Crockett to Richmond, where it is loaded onto railroad freight cars.

Carquinez Scenic Drive

This sinuous two-lane road carries you high above the south side of the Carquinez Strait. There are several places to safely pull off the road and look down on the passing maritime traffic. Old ferries, oil terminals, and Port Costa are the highlights of the drive.

Martinez

At the end of North Court Street are a marina, the ferryboat *Fresno*, and a public fishing pier. The fishing pier is a good place to watch ships coming and going at the busy Port of Benicia across the Strait. Exxon tankers, lumber, and automobile ships are common here. To the east of the marina on the Martinez side is another active oil terminal where tankers can be seen.

Avon

East of Martinez on Waterfront Road, is a large petroleum-receiving facility. The tankers tie up to a pier outside the marsh. Oil is pumped from the tankers into pipes and on to the refinery.

Across Suisun Bay is the Maritime Administration Reserve Fleet. Most of these ships date from World War II, and are kept for their potential value to national defense. It's worth remembering when looking at the Reserve Fleet that during World War II old sailing ships were put into service carrying cargo.

Port Chicago

This is a Navy ammunition depot. During the Viet Nam War it was quite active, and it was frequently possible to see ammunition ships at its piers. Now, ship's visits are much less frequent.

Antioch

There is a public fishing pier on the river in downtown Antioch. The pier is a good place to watch ships and barges bound into and out of Stockton, as well as the many recreational boats that use the Sacramento/San Joaquin River Delta.

The marinas under the Antioch Bridge are filled with classic power boats.

125

Index

Abbreviations: shipping schedule, 17; engines, 20; ship's markings, 23; supertankers, 25; Navy, 44
Agua Vista Park, 117
Aircraft carrier, 44, 46
Alameda, 38, 46, 70, 73, 120
Alameda Marina, 120
Alameda, Port of, 16
Alameda Yacht Harbor, 120
Alaska, 63
Alaska Packer ships, 92, 93, 119, 120
Albacore trolling, 83
Alcatraz, 79, 113
Alma, 94, 113
American River, 59
Ammunition ship, 44, 48
Anchorage, 17, 24, 28, 66, 68, 115, 117
Angel Island, ferry, 78, 80, 122
Angel Island State Park, 77, 78, 122
Antioch, 125
Army Corps of Engineers, 56
Army Corps of Engineers Bay Model, 122

Army Street Terminal, 69
Atchison, Topeka and Santa Fe Railroad, 57
Avon, 125
Ayala Cove, 122

Bait fishing, 88, 89
Balclutha, 93, 114
Barge anatomy, 60
Barge 450-1, 63
Barges, 53, 54, 60-63, 119, 124
Bar Pilots, 64, 65, 115
Bay Model, 122
Benicia, 28, 38, 125
Benicia, Port of, 16, 125
Bethlehem Steel Shipyard, 16, 117
Bitts, 51
Blackhaw, 76
Blooper, 104
Boat, definition, 9
Boatwatching, 9, 111-125
Bows, types of, 10, 18, 60
Bow thruster, 22, 34, 73
Brailed, 88
Break-bulk cargo carriers; see Cargo, break-bulk
Buccaneer, 89
Bull's-nose, 51, 57
Bunkering, 55, 63
Buoy tender, 76

Cable tending barge, 117
California Maritime Academy, 124
California: Pacific Mail Steamship, 20
California: pilot boat, 65
California Pilot, 66
Canal Boulevard, Richmond, 123-124
Cape Carter, 74
Cape Horners, 93, 113
Capstan, 51
Car carriers, 38, 39, 117, 124, 125
Cargo, bag bulk, 30
Cargo, break-bulk, 30, 114, 119
Cargo carriers, dry, 36
Cargo carriers, general, 30, 37
Cargo carriers, liquid, 24, 120. See also Tankers
Cargo, palletized, 30
Carpenter, 44, 47
Carquinez Scenic Drive, 125
Carriers, specialized, 38
Castro Point, 123
Catamaran, 106
Catboat, 104
Catenary, 51
Charles Van Damm, 77, 122
Charter cruises, 80
Chevron California, 26
Chevron Oregon, 26

Chevron tankers, 21, 26, 27, 123
China Basin, 116
Chinese Junk, 106
City of Oakland (fireboat), 118
Cliff House, 111
Clipper ships, 8, 21
Coast Guard, 72-76, 119, 120
Coast Guard Cutters, 19, 73, 74, 118
Coast Guard Station, Fort Point, 112
Cofferdam, 24
Colorado, 37
Comanche, 76
Container ships, 31, 32, 36, 37, 38, 116, 117
Convertible, 110
Coyote, 69
Crab boats, 90-91
Crab pots, 90
Cranes, 70, 124
Cranes, gantry, 32, 33, 42, 119
Crockett, 60, 125
Crowley Maritime Corporation, 53, 54, 58, 63, 70, 119
Crown-Zellerbach, 116
Cruise ships, 40, 114
Cutter, 104. See also Coast Guard Cutter

DB 300, 70
Deckhouse, 50, 53, 59
Definitions (salty), 10-11
Delta Lines, 42, 116
Destroyer, 44, 47
Displacement, 22-23
Dock Cafe, 120
Dolphin P. Rempp, 116
Draft, 10, 23
Draggers, 86-87
Drag net, 86-87
Drake, 65
Drawbridge, 116
Dry dock, floating, 16, 117, 118

Eagle, 71
Eileen D., 83
Encinal Terminal, 120
Engines, 20-21, 108; Diesel, 20-21; Electric, 21; Gas turbine, 21, 26, 73; Nuclear, 21, 45, 46; Steam turbine, 20, 25, 34, 37, 40, 42
Enterprise, 44, 46
Esther Louise, 84
Estuary Park, 118-119
Eureka, 77, 95-96, 113
Evans Radio Dock, 120
Excel, 48
Express, 109
Exxon Galveston, 29
Exxon Newark, 27

Fairleads, 51
Farallon Islands, 111
Feluccas, 81, 106
Fenders, 49-50, 59, 120
Ferries, 77-78, 95-96, 113, 115, 122, 125
Ferrocement, 101
Ferry Building, 77, 115
Fiberglass, 101
Fireboats, 67, 115, 118, 120
Fish and Game, 72
Fisherman's Wharf, 81, 87, 113
Fishery Conservation Limit, 73
Fishing boats, 81-91, 113, 120, 121
Flopper stoppers, 82
Flying bridge, 109, 110
Foresail, 104
Forestay, 104
Fort Mason, 112
Fort Point, 111
Fourth (4th) Street, Richmond, 124
Franciscan Restaurant, 113
Frank White, 62
Freighters, 30, 36
Friendship, 38
Fresno, 125

Gaff rigs, 106
Gangion, 85
Gantry cranes. See Cranes, gantry

George Miller Jr. Park, 123
Golden Bear, 124
Golden Gate, 78
Golden Gate Bridge, 115, 121
Golden Gate Ferry Landing, 115
Golden Gate National Recreation Area (GGNRA) 79, 112,121
Golden Gate Transit, 77, 115
Gold Rush, 8
Grand Street, Alameda, 120
Greenpeace, 114
Gurdies, 82

Harbor Emperor, 79
Harbor King, 79
Harbor Prince, 79
Harbor Princess, 79
Harbor Queen, 79
Harbor Tourist, 79
Harbor Tours, 77, 79, 113, 120
Harbor Tug and Barge, 120
Harbor tugs, 55-58, 121
Hawaiian Enterprise, 32
Hawaiian Progress, 32
Hawser, 52
Hay-scow schooners, 94-95, 113
"H" Bitts, 51
Heaving lines, 52
Hercules, 100, 113
Historical ships, 92-99, 113

Hornblower Party Yachts, 80
Hulls: Pleasure boats, 101, 108; Tugs, 49
Hybrid ships, 37
Hyde Street Pier, 77, 81, 95, 96, 113

Icebreakers, 72
Idaho, 37
Inland Pilot, 66
Inland Seas, 71
Islais Creek Channel, 17, 117
Issaquah, 77, 122

Jack Jr., 87
Jack London, 118
Jack London Square, 118-119
Jet drive, 68, 77, 108, 122
Jib, 104
Johnny T., 91

Keels, pleasure boats, 103
Ketch, 105
Kiska, 48
Klamath, 77, 115
Kort nozzles, 59

Lampara net boat, 88-89
Larkspur Ferry Terminal, 122-123
Las Plumas, 69
Lateen rig, 106
Lime Point, Lime Point Light, 121

Liners, 30, 40
Lines, 52
Lobos, 56
Loch Lomond Marina, 123
Long lining, 85-86
Lurline, 35

McNears Beach, 123
Maine, 34
Mallard, 66
Manhattan, 28
Manuel Mejia, 30
Mare Island Naval Shipyard, 45, 124
Marin, 77
Marin County, 121-124
Marine Ecological Institute, 71
Marine Exchange, 17
Mariner Square, Alameda, 73, 118, 120
Mariner II, 80
Mariner Yacht Charters, 80
Maritime Administration Reserve Fleet, 125
Maritime Museum, 92, 112
Markings, ships, 23
Marriott Inn, 80
Martinez, 125
Master Mariners Regatta, 94
Masts, numbers of (sailboats), 104-105
Matsonia, 35
Matson Navigation Company, 32, 35

Meatball Bait Company, 89
Merchant Marine, 124
Merchant shipping, 13-42
Merritt Shipyard, 63, 70, 118
Michigan, 37
Middle Harbor Park, 117-118
Minesweeper, 48, 71
Mission Rock terminal, 117
Monkey's fist, 52
Monterey Clipper, 81
Motor lifeboat, 75
Muir Beach Overlook, 121
Multihulls, 106

Nanook Carrier, 61
Nanoose Carrier, 61
National Maritime Museum, 92, 112
Nautilus, 45
Naval Supply Center, 117
Navy, 43-48, 123, 124, 125
Navy oceanographic and research ships, 71
Navy ship names, 43, 44
Ninth (9th) Avenue Terminal, Oakland, 119
Nordpol, 31
Norman pins, 51
North Bay, 124-125

Oakland, 33, 34, 35, 96, 117-119
Oakland, Port of, 15
Ocean Films, Ltd., 71
Ocean Trust Foundation, 71
Oil, 24, 25, 123, 124, 125

Oil spills, 68, 113
Opening Day, 122
Oregon, 63
Otter boards, 86

Pacific Dry Dock, 119
Pacific Queen, 93
Pacific Telephone and
    Telegraph, 117
PAD (Pacific Australia Direct
    Line), 34
Panama, 56
Pasha, 124
Passenger vessels, 30,
    40-42, 77, 114
Patrick Henry, 43
Paul P. Hastings, 57, 117
Pelican Harbor, 121
Phoenix, 67, 115
Pier 7, 65, 115
Pier 9, 66, 114
Piers 19-27, 114
Pier 22½, 115
Pier 28, 116
Pier 30-32, 116
Pier 31-33, 114
Pier 35, 114
Pier 36-38, 116
Pier 39, 114
Pier 42, 71
Pier 48, 116
Pier 52, 117
Pilots, 64, 115
Pleasure boats, 101-110
Plimsoll lines, 23

Point Barrow, 74
Point Bonita Lighthouse, 111
Point Molate Beach Park,123
Port Chicago, 125
Ports, 15-16
Portsmouth, 43
Portview Park, 117
Power (pleasure boats), 108
Powerboats, 108-110
President McKinley, 33
Propellers, 21-22
Push knees, 59, 61

Queensland, 39
Quinns Lighthouse, 120

Raccoon, 69
Raccoon Strait, 122
Red and White Fleet, 79, 80
Redrock Marina, 123
Red Stack, 58, 115, 120
Reduction gears, 20
Redwood City, Port of, 15-16
Refrigerator ship, 30
Research vessels, 71
Reserve Fleet, 125
Richmond, 38, 39, 57,
    123-124
Richmond Long Wharf, 17,
    24, 123
Richmond, Port of, 15
Rope, 49, 52
Ro/Ro, 19, 34, 36
Royal Star, 79, 80
Royal Viking Star, 41
Rush, 73

Sacramento, Port of, 15
Sailboats, 102-108
Sails, 102, 104, 105, 106
Saint Francis Yacht Club, 94,
    112
Salmon trolling, 81, 82, 113,
    119
San Francisco, 38, 111-117
San Francisco, ferry, 77, 78
San Francisco, pilot boat, 64
San Francisco, submarine,
    45
San Francisco, Port of, 15
San Francisco, Monument to
    USS, 111
San Rafael Channel, 123
Santa Fe Railroad, 116, 123
Santa Mercedes, 42, 115
Sausalito, 77, 78, 89, 96,
    121-122
Schedule of shipping, 17
Schooners, 105
Scomas, 113
Scow barge, 62
Screw, 22
Sea Horse, 58
Sea Lion, 53
Sea Swift, 54
Seawolf, 45
Sedan, 110
Ship, definition, 9
Shipping schedule, 17
Shipyards, 16, 117

Sidewheelers, 20, 21, 95-96
Siegfried Eagle, 58
Siegfried Tiger, 58
Skate, 85, 86
Sloop, 104
Smith-Rice #4, 70
Sonoma, 77
Southern Pacific Railroad, 96
Spill Spoiler, 68, 113
Spinnaker, 104
Sport Fisherman, 109
Standard Oil, 24-25, 26, 27
Star of Alaska, 93
Steam schooner, 97-98,
    113, 116
Sterns, types of, 19
Stockton, Port of, 15-16
Stolt Sincerity, 29
Submarines, 43, 44, 45, 71
Supertankers, 25

Tankers, 24-29, 120, 123,
    124, 125
Thayer, 98-99, 113
Three island ships: Tankers,
    25; Dry cargo, 36
Tiburon, 77, 122
Todd Shipyard, 16, 118
Tonnage, types of, 23
Tow boats, 59, 115, 124
Towing barges, 61
Towing winches, 50, 51, 58
Tramps, 30, 31
Trawlers: fishing, 86;
    pleasure, 110

Tri-Cabin, 110
Trident Restaurant, 122
Trimaran, 106
Triple A Shipyard, 16
Trolling poles, 81, 82, 83
Tugboats, 49-59, 64, 76,
    100, 114, 115, 116, 118,
    119
Tug, hull, 49
Tuna, 72

Ukiah, 95
Universal Wing, 39
Utility boat, 75

Vallejo, 124
Victoria Station, 120
Vista Point, 121
Vital statistics key, 10-11

Waldo Point, 122
Walking Beam, 96
Wapama, 97, 113
Water taxis, 66, 113, 114
Western Pacific Railroad, 69,
    100
Western Panther, 57
Western Tug and Barge, 58,
    124
Whales, Grey, 121
Winches, 51, 52, 58
Workboats, 64-76
Wyoming, 37

Yachts, 121
Yawl, 105